Cockney COOKBOOK

Tasty East End Grub

 CATHERINE ATKINSON

foulsham

LONDON • NEW YORK • TORONTO • SYDNEY

foulsham

The Publishing House, Bennetts Close, Cippenham,
Berkshire, SL1 5AP, England

Other books in the series:
Traditional Scottish Cookery by Sheila Macrae
Traditional Irish Cookery by Carmel Kavenagh

ISBN 0-572-02757-5

Printed in Great Britain by The Bath Press, Bath

Contents

Introduction

F ew Londoners remain in the city for long; they move in because of job opportunities and high salaries, then move on and out. The great exception to this is the proud cockney. True cockneys are small in number, for to claim the name, one must be born within the sound of Bow Bells, which ring out from the church of St Mary-le-Bow. This area was once the poorest part of London and cockneys relied on their quick wits and fierce loyalty to one another for survival.

They even developed a language of their own to protect them from outsiders – the so-called 'rhyming slang', which substitutes rhyming phrases for words, and then uses only the non-rhyming part. Thus, 'plates of meat' is substituted for 'feet' and then shortened to 'plates', as in 'My plates are killing me'. Some terms have become part of everyday language throughout the country, such as 'bread', meaning money, which originates from the rhyming slang expression 'bread and honey'.

Cockneys were often physically small, due to poor nutrition, and their size, together with their boldness, drew comparison to the cock sparrow, which is where the name 'cockney' comes from.

Many cockneys were traditional market traders and vast numbers also worked in the London docks, which flourished during the nineteenth century to become one of the greatest ports in the world. The cockney docker was renowned for his strength and hard-working nature, as well as for his colourful language.

Food for these hardworking folk had to be cheap, filling and nourishing. Traditional cockney fare included gelatinous dishes such as pigs' trotters, brawn and jellied eels. Food was always well flavoured, never bland: saveloys served with pickles, smoky kippers and inexpensive seafood such as whelks and cockles, generously doused in vinegar, were favourites. Even drinks had to be strong; tea brewed to the colour of black treacle, dry London gin and dark bitter stout.

There were outside influences too, particularly that of the Jews who escaped to England from the pogroms of Eastern Europe and arrived by cattle boats to settle in the area around the docklands.

The commercial side of the docks has now disappeared. The Port of London, once vital for importing nearly all of the goods into Britain, has declined in the face of competition from airlines, containers and more recently the Channel Tunnel. However, it now flourishes with new businesses, such as the Canary Wharf development, and has become a desirable place to live, with many warehouses being converted into spacious flats with fabulous views over the Thames.

Nevertheless, traditional cockney cookery has stood the test of time. Its distinctive bright, uncomplicated style survives, as the dishes I have chosen for this book show.

Rhyming slang

Cockney rhyming slang covers almost every subject you can think of, and an amazing amount of it is related to food or drink.

Rhyming slang	Meaning
Apple cider	Spider
Apple fritter	Bitter (beer)
Apples and pears	Stairs
Bag of fruit	Suit (of clothes)
Baked beans	Jeans
Bath bun	Son
Biscuits and cheese	Knees
Bread and honey	Money
Brussels sprout	Boy scout
Coffee and cocoa	Say so, as in 'I should cocoa'
Currant bun	Sun
Ham and eggs	Legs
Hampstead Heath	Teeth
Hot cross bun	Run, as in 'on the run'
Loaf of bread	Head, as in 'use your loaf'
Meat pie	Fly
Mince pies	Eyes
North and south	Mouth
Plates of meat	Feet
Pork pies	Lies, hence 'porkies'
Potatoes in the mould	Cold hence 'taters'
Rabbit and pork	Talk
Sausage and mash	Cash, hence 'I haven't got a sausage'
Stewed prune	Tune
Syrup of fig	Wig
Tea leaf	Thief
Treacle tart	Sweetheart

The rhyming slang equivalents for items of food and drink are equally colourful, but harder to guess.

Food	Rhyming slang
Ale (light)	Silent night
Army and navy	Gravy
Banana	Gertie Gitana
Beer	Pig's ear
Brandy	Fine and dandy
Bread	Uncle Fred
Butter	Cough and splutter
Cake	Give and take
Cheese	Cough and sneeze
Coffee	Everton toffee
Drink	Tiddlywink, hence 'tiddly'
Gin	Vera Lynn
Jelly	Mother Kelly
Kipper	Jack the Ripper
Lunch	Judy and Punch
Onions	Corns and bunions
Pear	Teddy bear
Pickle (to eat)	Slap and tickle
Rice	Three blind mice
Scotch	Gold watch
Sherry	Woolwich ferry
Soup	Loop the loop
Tea	Rosie Lee
Toast	Holy Ghost

Notes on the Recipes

- Quantities are given in metric, imperial and American measures. Follow one set only.

- American terms are given in brackets.

- All spoon measurements are level: 1 tsp = 5 ml;
  1 tbsp = 15 ml.

- Eggs are medium unless otherwise state.

- Always wash, peel, core and seed, if necessary, fresh foods before use. Ensure that all produce is as fresh as possible and in good condition.

- Seasoning and the use of strongly flavoured ingredients, such as onions and garlic, are very much a matter of personal taste. Taste the food as you cook and adjust seasoning to suit your own taste.

- Always preheat the oven (unless using a fan-assisted oven) and cook on the centre shelf unless otherwise specified. Ovens vary, so cooking times have to be approximate. For fan ovens, reduce temperatures by about 10°C for every 100°C and times by 10 minutes for each hour **above** the first hour.

- All preparation and cooking times are approximate and should be used as a guide only.

Meat

L ondon's meat market is to be found in the heart of the East End, at Smithfield. From the early hours of the morning, Smithfield market is buzzing with activity. Meat from throughout Britain and abroad comes to the capital's greatest wholesale market – still the largest in Europe – where over 3,000 people buy and sell the 350,000 tons of meat that pass through each year. Porters help shift the goods from sellers to buyers and by mid-morning stalls are cleared and hosed down ready for another day and workers gather in local, specially licensed public houses, which serve hearty English breakfasts, often accompanied by a pint of beer.

Smithfield was not always purely a meat market; in Tudor times it was a place of public execution, before it became a live cattle and horse market, and, in Victorian times, an abbatoir.

East Enders are famous for their love of jellied meat, whether brawn or pigs' trotters; these nutritious, inexpensive dishes in rich jelly are now to be found on the menus of even the most prestigious restaurants. Pie and mash shops serving traditional meat pies with parsley sauce are still to be found in the docklands area, alongside the smart Continental and Asian restaurants and American burger bars.

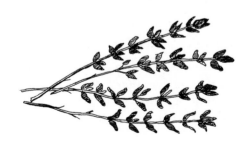

Steak and Kidney Pudding

*This is probably one of the best-known British dishes. In less
prosperous days, the long steaming needed for these puddings
tenderised cheaper cuts of meat – the cost of the fuel needed
was not a problem as the kitchen range would be burning all
day in the colder winter months. St George is of course the patron
saint of England, celebrated by many patriotic East Enders on
23 April (which is also Shakespeare's birthday).*

SERVES 6

45 ml/3 tbsp plain (all-purpose) flour
Salt and freshly ground black pepper
900 g/2 lb braising steak, trimmed and cubed
225 g/8 oz beef or pork kidneys, cored and chopped
30 ml/2 tbsp vegetable oil
25 g/1 oz/2 tbsp butter or margarine
1 large onion, thinly sliced
225 g/8 oz field mushrooms
15 ml/1 tbsp Worcestershire sauce
250 ml/8 fl oz/1 cup beef stock
250 ml/8 fl oz/1 cup brown ale or stout
1 bay leaf
For the pastry (paste):
225 g/8 oz/2 cups self-raising (self-rising) flour
75 g/3 oz/¾ cup shredded (chopped) beef suet
120–150 ml/4 fl oz–¼ pt/½–⅔ cup cold water

1 Season the plain flour with salt and pepper, then toss
the steak and kidneys in the flour to coat. Heat half the oil
and butter or margarine in a large, heavy-based saucepan,
then cook the meat in batches until well browned. Set aside.

2 Add the remaining oil and butter or margarine and
gently cook the onion for 5 minutes, then add the mushrooms
and continue cooking, stirring frequently, until soft and
beginning to colour. Return the meat to the pan, then add
the Worcestershire sauce, stock, ale or stout and bay leaf.

3 Slowly bring to the boil, then reduce the heat to very low. Cover and simmer gently for 1¼ hours or until the meat is tender. Taste and adjust the seasoning if necessary. Discard the bay leaf.

4 To make the pastry, sift the self-raising flour into a bowl, stir in the suet, then add enough of the water to make a soft dough. Roll out two-thirds of the dough on a lightly floured surface and use to line a greased 1.75 litre/3 pt/ 7½ cup pudding basin, leaving any extra pastry hanging over the sides.

5 Spoon the steak and kidney mixture into the pastry-lined bowl and brush the top edge with water. Roll out the remaining pastry to make a lid and press firmly to seal.

6 Cover the basin with greaseproof (waxed) paper, pleated in the centre. Cover with foil and tie firmly with string. Place in a saucepan and pour in enough boiling water to come two-thirds of the way up the sides of the bowl. Cover and simmer gently for 2 hours, adding more boiling water as needed.

7 Remove the pudding and allow to stand for 5 minutes. Take off the wrappings, loosen the edges with a round-bladed knife and turn out on to a warmed plate.

⏱ **Preparation and cooking time:** 3½ hours

► **Cook's tip**
For a Steak and Kidney Pie, spoon the filling into a 1.2 litre/ 2 pt/5 cup pie dish, roll out the suet pastry and use to cover. Bake in a preheated oven at 180°C/350°F/gas mark 4 for 45 minutes or until the pastry is slightly risen and golden.

> *St George he was for England,*
> *And, before he killed the dragon,*
> *He drank a pint of English ale*
> *Out of an English flagon.*
> GK Chesterton

Pie and Mash

░░

Throughout Edwardian and Victorian times and right up until the 1960s, there were dozens of 'pie and eel' shops all over the East End of London. Currently they are undergoing a revival, although they are no longer the cheap and spartan eating houses once only frequented by the working classes. The pies contain chunks of eel or meat, or sometimes minced (ground) beef, and are served with mashed potatoes and a generous helping of parsley sauce, known as 'liquor'. Fruit pies or steamed puddings and custard are usually on offer as a second course for those with very large appetites!

SERVES 6

700 g/1½ lb lean minced beef
1 large onion, finely chopped
250 ml/8 fl oz/1 cup good-quality beef stock
1 bay leaf
5 ml/1 tsp cornflour (cornstarch)
2.5 ml/½ tsp made English mustard
10 ml/2 tsp Worcestershire sauce
A little cold water
Salt and freshly ground black pepper
For the pastry (paste):
225 g/8 oz/2 cups plain (all-purpose) flour
A pinch of salt
100 g/4 oz/1 cup butter or half white vegetable fat and half butter
45–60 ml/3–4 tbsp cold water
Beaten egg or milk, to glaze
For the parsley sauce:
25 g/1 oz/2 tbsp butter or margarine
25 g/1 oz/¼ cup plain (all-purpose) flour
450 ml/¾ pt/2 cups milk
Salt and freshly ground black pepper
45 ml/3 tbsp chopped fresh parsley

1 Put the minced beef in a large, preferably non-stick, saucepan and cook over a medium heat in its own fat until beginning to brown. Add the onion and cook, stirring frequently, for a further 5 minutes until softened.

2 Add the stock and bay leaf, cover and simmer for 20 minutes. Mix the cornflour, mustard, Worcestershire sauce and 10 ml/2 tsp cold water together. Stir into the beef mixture and season with salt and pepper.

3 Simmer, uncovered, for 20 minutes or until the mixture is very thick. Stir frequently towards the end to prevent the mixture from sticking. Leave to cool. Discard the bay leaf.

4 Meanwhile, make the pastry. Sift the flour and salt into a bowl, then rub in the fat until the mixture resembles fine breadcrumbs. Sprinkle over the water, then mix together to make a firm dough.

5 Lightly knead the pastry on a floured surface for a few seconds until smooth. Wrap in clingfilm (plastic wrap) and chill for 20 minutes.

6 Put a heavy baking (cookie) sheet in the oven and preheat to 200°C/400°F/gas mark 6. Roll out slightly more than half of the pastry and use to line a 25 cm/10 in pie plate.

7 Spoon in the filling, putting a pie funnel in the middle if you have one. Moisten the edge with water, then roll out the remaining pastry and cover the filling. Trim and flute the edges. Re-roll the pastry trimmings and use to decorate.

8 Brush with beaten egg or milk to glaze. Make two or three steam holes in the top. Place on the hot baking sheet and bake in the preheated oven for 20 minutes, then reduce the oven temperature to 180°C/350°F/gas mark 4 and bake for a further 20 minutes or until the pastry is golden brown and crisp.

9 While the pie is cooking, make the parsley sauce. Melt the butter or margarine in a saucepan, stir in the flour and cook, stirring, for a minute. Remove from the heat and gradually add the milk, whisking constantly. Season to taste.

10 Return to the heat and cook, stirring, until thickened and smooth. Stir in the parsley and simmer for 2 more minutes. Serve hot with the pie.

☉ **Preparation and cooking time:** 2 hours

Steak and Oyster Pie

In the nineteenth century, oysters, which were then cheap and plentiful, were added to many meat dishes, such as this pie. In the twentieth century, however, the oyster beds stopped producing because of over-fishing and increasing pollution, and oysters became the province of the rich. Eventually, they were replaced by pieces of kidney or sometimes by mushrooms (see Steak and Kidney Pie, page 11).

SERVES 6

25 g/1 oz/2 tbsp butter or margarine
1 onion, sliced
900 g/2 lb lean chuck steak, cut into 2.5 cm/1 in cubes
30 ml/2 tbsp plain (all-purpose) flour
Salt and freshly ground black pepper
30 ml/2 tbsp vegetable oil
225 g/8 oz baby button mushrooms
1 bay leaf
A sprig of thyme
450 ml/¾ pt/2 cups beef stock
18 oysters, opened
450 g/1 lb puff pastry (paste)
1 egg, lightly beaten, to glaze

1 Melt the butter or margarine in an ovenproof casserole (Dutch oven) and gently cook the onion for 10 minutes until softened. Remove and set aside.

2 Toss the meat in the flour, seasoned with a little salt and pepper. Add the oil to the casserole and fry (sauté) the meat in batches until well browned all over.

3 Return the onion to the casserole. Add the mushrooms, bay leaf, thyme and stock. Cover and put in a preheated oven at 150°C/300°F/gas mark 2 for 1½ hours or until the meat is tender. Remove the bay leaf and thyme.

4 Transfer the meat, onions and mushrooms to a
1.5 litre/2½ pt/6 cup pie dish. Boil the meat juices in the
casserole until reduced to about 300 ml/½ pt/1¼ cups. Pour
over the meat and leave to cool. Stir in the oysters and their
juices.

5 Put a baking (cookie) tray in the oven and increase the
temperature to 220°C/425°F/gas mark 7. Roll out the pastry
on a lightly floured surface to a round 5 cm/2 in larger than
the pie dish. Cut off a 2.5 cm/1 in strip from around the
edge. Moisten the rim of the pie dish and attach the strip.

6 Moisten the top of the strip with water, place the
remaining pastry over the top and press the edges together
to seal. Trim and flute, then use the pastry trimmings to
decorate the pie, if liked. Glaze with beaten egg and make a
steam-hole with a skewer.

7 Bake for 10 minutes, then reduce the oven
temperature to 200°C/400°F/gas mark 6 and bake for a
further 20–25 minutes or until the pastry is well risen and a
dark golden brown.

⏲ **Preparation and cooking time:** 2¾ hours

➤ **Cook's tip**
Use an extra 100 g/4 oz mushrooms instead of the oysters, if
preferred.

> *Poverty and oysters always seem to go together.*
> Charles Dickens, *Pickwick Papers*

Bangers in Rich Onion Gravy

In the East End you'll still find butchers who sell only sausages. The range they offer, which includes many seasonal specialities, is overwhelming and, following current food trends, most are made with natural skins and contain no artificial additives. A large vegetarian selection is also offered as well as saveloys, smoked pork sausages that are still sold in fish and chip shops. Not so long ago, large copper saveloy heaters were a common sight in London pubs where these tasty sausages were kept hot and ready to eat.

SERVES 4

15 ml/1 tbsp sunflower oil
450 g/1 lb good-quality pork sausages
175 g/6 oz smoked streaky bacon in a piece, cut into small cubes
15 g/½ oz/1 tbsp butter or margarine
2 onions, thinly sliced
10 ml/2 tsp plain (all-purpose) flour
300 ml/½ pt/1¼ cups beef or vegetable stock
2.5 ml/½ tsp made English mustard
1 bay leaf
Salt and freshly ground black pepper

1 Heat the oil in a large frying pan (skillet) over a medium heat and brown the sausages all over. Remove from the pan and set aside.

2 Add the bacon cubes to the pan and fry (sauté) over a high heat until brown and crispy. Transfer to the plate with the sausages, using a slotted spoon and leaving the fat behind.

3 Add the butter or margarine and sliced onions to the pan and gently cook for 12–15 minutes until very soft and golden brown, stirring frequently towards the end of cooking time.

4 Sprinkle over the flour and stir in, then gradually add the stock. Bring to the boil, stirring all the time until thickened. Stir in the mustard, bay leaf and seasoning.

5 Return the sausages to the pan, cover and simmer gently for 20 minutes. Sprinkle with the bacon before serving.

🕐 **Preparation and cooking time:** 45 minutes

➤ **Cook's tip**
Serve the sausages with creamy mashed potato and some peas or beans.

Toad in the Hole

This dish of sausages baked in batter is universally enjoyed and although not exclusive to the East End, is extremely popular there. Use good-quality sausages, for the best results.

SERVES 4

15 ml/1 tbsp sunflower oil
450 g/1 lb pork sausages
100 g/4 oz/1 cup plain (all-purpose) flour
A pinch of salt
2 eggs
300 ml/½ pt/1¼ cups milk or a mixture of half water, half milk
Freshly ground black pepper

1 Use the oil to grease a small roasting tin (pan), then add the sausages. Cook in the oven at 220°C/425°F/gas mark 7 for 10 minutes until the sausages are lightly browned.

2 Meanwhile, sift the flour and salt into a mixing bowl and make a well in the middle. Whisk the eggs, milk and pepper together, then pour into the dry ingredients, and gradually mix together to make a batter.

3 Turn the sausages, then pour the batter over and immediately return to the oven. Reduce the oven temperature to 200°C/400°F/gas mark 6 and bake for a further 30 minutes or until the batter is well risen and golden brown. Serve straight away.

🕐 **Preparation and cooking time:** 45 minutes

Faggots with Creamy Pea Purée

Faggots, also sometimes more appealingly known as 'savoury ducks' or 'poor man's goose', are a cross between a sausage and a pâté. Originally an ideal way of using up the bits of offal after a pig was killed, they can be made with whatever offal and cheap cuts your butcher may have. Caul fat is traditionally used to enclose each faggot and to keep it moist during cooking; this can sometimes be bought from an old-fashioned butcher, but it is quite hard to find. You can simply shape and cook the faggots without it. A slice of pease pudding or a purée made of dried peas is the traditional accompaniment to faggots. Here I have made a more modern version of the purée with fresh or frozen peas.

SERVES 4

225 g/8 oz caul fat (optional)
450 g/1 lb pork cuts, such as belly pork, heart and liver
15 ml/1 tbsp sunflower oil
1 small onion, very finely chopped
50 g/2 oz/1 cup fresh white breadcrumbs
10 ml/2 tsp chopped fresh sage
A pinch of freshly grated nutmeg
1 egg, lightly beaten
Salt and freshly ground black pepper
120 ml/4 fl oz/½ cup beef stock
For the Creamy Pea Purée:
25 g/1 oz/2 tbsp butter or margarine
1 small onion, very finely chopped
350 g/12 oz/3 cups fresh shelled or frozen peas
120 ml/4 fl oz/½ cup double (heavy) cream
120 ml/4 fl oz/½ cup vegetable stock
Salt and freshly ground black pepper

1 Put the caul fat, if using, in a bowl and pour over enough warm water to cover. Leave to soften while preparing the meat.

2 Remove any fat or gristle from the meat, then mince (grind) finely. (You can ask your butcher to do this for you.)

3 Heat the oil in a large pan and gently fry (sauté) the onion for 5 minutes. Add the meat and fry over a medium heat until just cooked.

4 Remove from the heat, lift out the meat with a slotted spoon and reserve the juices. Allow the meat to cool for a few minutes, then add the breadcrumbs, sage, nutmeg, egg, salt and pepper. Mix together thoroughly.

5 Drain the caul fat, if using, spread it out and cut into 13 cm/5 in squares. Divide the meat between the squares, then wrap to make ovals, gathering the caul around the meat, or simply shape the meat into ovals. Place them in an ovenproof dish with the seams underneath.

6 Pour the reserved meat juices and the stock over the faggots. Cover the dish with foil, then bake at 180°C/350°F/ gas mark 4 for 20 minutes. Remove the foil and bake for a further 20 minutes until browned.

7 Meanwhile, make the pea purée. Melt the butter or margarine in a saucepan and gently fry the onion for 10 minutes until soft and just starting to turn golden.

8 Add the peas, cream and stock and simmer for 8–10 minutes or until the peas are tender and the liquid has reduced by about half. Season generously with salt and pepper.

9 Transfer to a blender or food processor and process to a rough purée. Return to the saucepan and gently reheat until piping hot.

10 Serve with the faggots.

⊕ **Preparation and cooking time:** 1 hour

➤ **Cook's tip**
If cooking the faggots without caul fat, brush with 15 ml/ 1 tbsp sunflower oil after removing the foil to brown (see step 6).

Boiled Beef and Carrots

This is the stuff of the famous music hall song (see below). 'Derby Kell' is short for 'Derby Kelly' – cockney rhyming slang for 'belly'.

SERVES 6

1.5 kg/3 lb lean salted silverside or brisket
2 bay leaves
A sprig of thyme
6 black peppercorns
1 onion, quartered
1 celery stick, roughly chopped
18 small carrots, scrubbed

1 Soak the beef in cold water for at least 3 hours, or overnight if preferred. Rinse, then tie at 2.5 cm/1 in intervals with fine string.

2 Put the beef in a saucepan in which it just fits. Add the herbs, peppercorns, onion and celery. Bring to the boil, then reduce the heat, part-cover with a lid and simmer very gently for 2 hours.

3 Add the carrots and simmer for a further 30 minutes or until tender. Lift out the beef and carrots on to a serving plate, reserving the liquid, then cover and leave the meat to 'rest' for 10 minutes before carving.

4 Skim and discard the fat from the cooking liquid, then boil rapidly for 5 minutes to reduce it slightly. Strain into a jug and serve as a gravy with the meat and carrots.

⏲ **Preparation and cooking time:** 3 hours plus soaking

> *Boiled beef and carrots, boiled beef and carrots.*
> *That's the stuff for your Derby Kell.*
> *Makes you fat and keeps you well.*
>
> Old music hall song

Traditional Cold Meat Terrine

Strong-flavoured meats, such as pigs' liver, and economical ones, like pork belly, have always been popular in East End cooking. Find a helpful butcher who will mince (grind) meat for you; otherwise chop it very finely, but do not use a food processor as the texture of the terrine should be slightly chunky, not smooth. Serve the sliced terrine with lots of crusty rye bread and pungent pickles.

SERVES 6–8

350 g/12 oz pork belly
350 g/12 oz beef
225 g/8 oz pigs' liver
225 g/8 oz smoked streaky bacon, rinded and finely chopped
45 ml/3 tbsp brandy
75 ml/5 tbsp white wine
4 juniper berries, crushed
5 ml/1 tsp dried thyme
Salt and freshly ground black pepper

1 Mince all the meats and put in a bowl with all the other ingredients. Mix thoroughly together. Cover and chill for 1 hour for the flavours to mingle, then mix again.

2 Spoon the mixture into a well-greased 900 g/2 lb terrine or loaf tin (pan), packing down well. Cover with the top with foil.

3 Stand the tin in a roasting tin and pour in enough boiling water to come about halfway up the sides. Bake in the oven at 150°C/300°F/gas mark 2 for 2 hours, or until the juices run clear when a skewer is pushed into the centre.

4 Remove the terrine or tin from the hot water and place on a cooling rack. Leave for 20 minutes, then weigh down with cans or weights. When cold, put in the fridge with the weights and leave to set firm overnight.

5 Serve cut the terrine into thick slices.

⏲ **Preparation and cooking time:** 2 hours plus marinating

Bartelmas Beef

In London, a huge fair dating back to 1133 used to be held at Smithfield meat market, in honour of St Bartholomew, the patron saint of butchers and tanners. The fair provided income for the nearby hospital of St Barts, but was banned in 1855 because it was thought it might encourage 'immoral behaviour'! This spiced brisket dish is an ideal joint for a cold buffet as it will keep for up to a week in the fridge. Long, slow simmering ensures that it will be beautifully tender.

SERVES 12

A piece of boned and rolled brisket, about 2–2.25 kg/4½–5 lb
5 ml/1 tsp black peppercorns
5 ml/1 tsp allspice berries
5 ml/1 tsp juniper berries
100 g/4 oz/1 cup coarse sea salt
2.5 ml/½ tsp ground cloves
10 ml/2 tsp dried thyme
1 onion, roughly chopped
1 celery stick, roughly chopped
1 large carrot, roughly chopped
2 bay leaves
A sprig of rosemary

1 Open out the joint of meat and pat it dry with kitchen paper (paper towels). Place in a large, shallow, glass or china dish. Crush the peppercorns, allspice and juniper berries coarsely, using a mortar and pestle or a coffee grinder.

2 Tip the ground spices into a bowl and add the salt, cloves and thyme. Mix well, then rub half this spice mixture over one side of the meat. Turn the meat over and rub in the remaining mixture.

3 Cover with clingfilm (plastic wrap) and place at the bottom of the fridge for 5 days. Turn the meat daily, spooning over the spices each time.

4 Lift out the beef and wipe off the marinade with kitchen paper. Re-roll and tie at 2.5 cm/1 in intervals with fine string.

5 Place the vegetables and fresh herbs in a pan, just large enough to fit the joint. Sit the meat on top, then pour in enough cold water to come just over halfway up the meat.

6 Bring to the boil, then reduce the heat, cover and cook gently for 2¼ hours, topping up with extra boiling water when necessary. Leave the meat to cool in the water – you can shorten the time this takes by placing the pan in a sink half-filled with cold water.

7 Lift the meat out and tightly wrap in foil. Put on a plate, then place a board on top and add a few heavy weights or cans on top to press the meat. Place in the fridge until well chilled. Serve cut into thin slices.

⏱ **Preparation and cooking time:** 2½ hours plus marinating

➤ **Cook's tip**
The stock can be saved and added to a soup or casserole. Use only a small amount though, as it will be very salty.

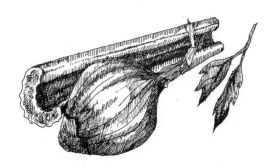

Stuffed Breast of Lamb with Root Vegetable Mash

This is an inexpensive but well-flavoured cut of meat. It can be somewhat fatty, so trim it well before using. The Root Vegetable Mash, a traditional accompaniment for this dish, is a good way of adding flavour to plain mashed potatoes and economises on fuel by cooking all the vegetables together in one saucepan.

SERVES 4

450 g/1 lb breast of lamb, boned
10 ml/2 tsp sunflower oil
1 small onion, very finely chopped
1 egg, beaten
50 g/2 oz/1 cup fresh white or wholemeal breadcrumbs
30 ml/2 tbsp chopped fresh mint
15 ml/1 tbsp chopped fresh parsley
15 ml/1 tbsp lemon juice
Salt and freshly ground black pepper
For the Root Vegetable Mash:
225 g/8 oz potatoes, cut into large chunks
225 g/8 oz swede (rutabaga), cut into chunks
225 g/8 oz carrots, thickly sliced
25 g/1 oz/2 tbsp butter or margarine
100 ml/3½ fl oz/scant ½ cup hot milk
Salt and freshly ground black pepper

1 Place the meat on a board and cut away excess fat.

2 Heat the oil in a frying pan (skillet) and gently cook the onion for 6–7 minutes or until softened, but not browned. Remove from the heat and leave until cool.

3 Add the beaten egg, breadcrumbs, mint, parsley and lemon juice. Season well with salt and pepper, then mix together to combine thoroughly.

4 Spread the stuffing out evenly over the meat, then roll up tightly, securing at 2.5 cm/1 in intervals with fine string.

5 Place the joint on a rack over a roasting tin (pan). Cover with foil and roast at 220°C/425°F/gas mark 7 for 30 minutes. Remove the foil, so that the meat can brown and cook for a further 20 minutes or until cooked to your liking.

6 Meanwhile, make the vegetable mash. Put the prepared vegetables in a saucepan and pour over just enough water to cover. Season with salt, bring to the boil and simmer for 20 minutes or until tender. Drain well.

7 Mash the vegetables in the pan with the butter or margarine, then gradually mash in the hot milk until smooth and creamy. Season with black pepper and extra salt if needed.

8 Remove the lamb from the oven, re-cover with foil and allow the joint to rest for 10 minutes, before carving and serving with the mash.

🕐 **Preparation and cooking time:** 1½ hours

➤ **Cook's tip**
You can, if you prefer, serve the lamb with roast potatoes.

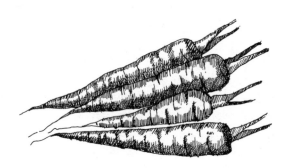

Lamb and Barley Stew with Parsley Dumplings

SERVES 4

30 ml/2 tbsp sunflower oil

2 rashers (slices) of smoked streaky bacon or lardons, rinded and chopped

15 g/½ oz/1 tbsp butter or margarine

1 large onion, chopped

30 ml/2 tbsp plain (all-purpose) flour

Salt and freshly ground black pepper

1 kg/2¼ lb boned leg or shoulder of lamb, trimmed and cut into 2.5 cm/1 in cubes

4 carrots, cut into 2.5 cm/1 in chunks

175 g/6 oz swede (rutabaga), cut into 2.5 cm/1 in chunks

2 celery sticks, thickly sliced

30 ml/2 tbsp pearl barley

5 ml/1 tsp chopped fresh thyme

1 bay leaf

450 ml/¾ pt/2 cups lamb or vegetable stock

For the Parsley Dumplings:

175 g/6 oz/1½ cups self-raising (self-rising) flour

A pinch of salt

A pinch of English mustard powder

75 g/3 oz/¾ cup shredded (chopped) beef or vegetable suet

45 ml/3 tbsp chopped fresh parsley

A little iced water, to bind

1 Heat 15 ml/1 tbsp of the oil in a large, flameproof casserole (Dutch oven) and fry (sauté) the bacon or lardons for a minute or so until lightly browned. Remove with a slotted spoon and set aside, leaving any fat in the casserole.

2 Add the butter or margarine and onion to the casserole and gently cook over a medium heat for 5 minutes until beginning to brown. Remove and add to the bacon.

3 Season the flour with salt and pepper and toss the lamb in the mixture. Heat the remaining oil in the casserole and fry the lamb until well browned on all sides. Return the bacon and onion to the casserole.

4 Add the carrots, swede, celery, barley, thyme, bay leaf and stock. Season with salt and pepper. Bring to the boil, then reduce the heat, cover and simmer very gently for 1½ hours, stirring occasionally towards the end.

5 Meanwhile, make the dumplings. Sift the flour, salt and mustard powder into a bowl and stir in the suet and parsley. Stir in just enough iced water to bind to a soft dough. Divide into 12 pieces and roll into balls with floured hands. Drop into the casserole, re-cover and simmer for a further 25–30 minutes or until well risen.

🕐 **Preparation and cooking time:** 2½ hours

➤ **Cook's tip**
After adding the dumplings, don't be tempted to check on them for at least 20 minutes, otherwise they may collapse.

A friendly swarry, consisting of a boiled leg of mutton with the usual trimmings.
Charles Dickens, *Pickwick Papers*

Raised Pork Pie

This crusty pie is made with hot-water pastry (paste) and is used for traditional cold pies, sometimes referred to as 'standing pies' because they hold their shape during and after cooking. Unlike shortcrust (basic pie crust) and puff pastry, hot-water crust can be moulded into shape without making it heavy and it can withstand a long cooking time. Here the pie is made in a tin (pan), but smaller ones are often made by moulding the pastry over greased jam jars, chilling to harden slightly, then inverting on to a baking (cookie) sheet before filling. Pork pies should be made at least 24 hours before serving to allow them to firm and to let the flavours develop.

SERVES 6

For the filling:
700 g/1½ lb minced (ground) pork
175 g/6 oz streaky bacon, rinded and chopped
1 small onion, grated or very finely chopped
30 ml/2 tbsp brandy
5 ml/1 tsp made English mustard
5 ml/1 tsp dried mixed herbs
Salt and freshly ground black pepper
1 sachet of aspic jelly

For the hot-water pastry:
350 g/12 oz/3 cups plain (all-purpose) flour
5 ml/1 tsp salt
100 g/4 oz/½ cup lard (shortening) or white vegetable fat
150 ml/¼ pt/⅔ cup water

1 Put all the filling ingredients except the aspic jelly in a bowl and mix together until thoroughly combined. Cover and set aside.

2 To make the pastry, sift the flour and salt into a bowl and make a well in the middle. Gently heat the lard or white vegetable fat and water in a small pan until the fat has melted. Pour into the well and mix together to make a soft dough.

3 Knead the pastry on a lightly floured surface for a few seconds until smooth. Cut off a quarter, wrap in clingfilm (plastic wrap) and set aside.

4 Roll out the rest of the pastry and use to line a deep 15 cm/6 in loose-bottomed round tin. Using a sharp knife, held at an angle away from the dish, trim off any excess pastry.

5 Put a baking tray in the oven and preheat to 200°C/ 400°F/gas mark 6. Spoon the meat mixture into the tin, packing down tightly. Roll out the reserved pastry to make a lid about 1 cm/½ in bigger than the tin. Brush the edges with water, position the lid in place, then press together to seal. Crimp the edges. Cut a small cross in the middle of the lid and fold back the corners to make a steam hole.

6 Put the pie on the hot baking sheet and bake for 20 minutes. Turn down the oven temperature to 180°C/ 350°F/gas mark 4 and bake for a further 1½ hours, covering the pie with foil towards the end of cooking time if it is browning too much.

7 After cooking, the filling in the pie will have shrunk slightly, leaving a gap between the pastry and filling. Leave the pie to cool for 1½ hours, then make up the aspic, following the packet instructions, but using only half the quantity of liquid. Slowly pour it through the steam-hole until full. Cool, then cover and chill overnight in the fridge. The pie will keep, wrapped, in the fridge for 4 days.

⏱ **Preparation and cooking time:** 2¼ hours

➤ **Cook's tip**
To test the seasoning of the pie, take a small spoonful of the raw filling mixture and gently fry (sauté) it until cooked through, then taste it and adjust the seasoning as necessary.

> *I stole some bread, some rind of cheese, about half a jar of mincemeat ..., some brandy from a stone bottle (which I decanted into a glass bottle) ... a meat bone with very little on it, and a beautiful round compact pork pie.*
> Charles Dickens, *Great Expectations*

Rabbit Casserole

Rabbits could once be bought for just a few pence and the cockney housewife would skin and cook them, then sell the skins and recoup most of the cost. Chicken joints can be cooked in the same way.

SERVES 4

12 small shallots
4 rabbit portions
175 g/6 oz/1½ cups cooked ham, cut into small cubes
2 carrots, sliced
600 ml/1 pt/2½ cups milk
1 bay leaf
A pinch of freshly grated nutmeg
Salt and freshly ground black pepper
15 g/½ oz/2 tbsp cornflour (cornstarch)
A little cold water
15 g/½ oz/1 tbsp butter or margarine
60 ml/4 tbsp chopped fresh parsley

1 Put the shallots in a bowl and pour over enough boiling water to cover. Leave for 5 minutes, then drain and briefly rinse under cold water. Peel off the skins.

2 Arrange the rabbit portions in an ovenproof casserole dish (Dutch oven) with the shallots, ham and carrots.

3 Bring the milk to the boil with the bay leaf, nutmeg, salt and pepper. Pour over the rabbit.

4 Cover with a lid or foil and bake at 180°C/350°F/gas mark 4 for 1 hour or until the rabbit and vegetables are tender. Transfer to a serving dish and keep warm.

5 Strain the milk into a saucepan. Blend the cornflour and water to a paste, stir into the milk and bring to the boil. Add the butter or margarine and simmer for 2 minutes, then stir in the parsley and simmer for 1 minute.

6 Taste the sauce and adjust the seasoning if necessary. Pour over the rabbit and vegetables and serve straight away.

⏱ **Preparation and cooking time:** 1½ hours

Ale-braised Oxtail

The brown ale, together with long, slow cooking, tenderises the rich meat in this dish.

SERVES 4

2 small oxtails, about 1.5 kg/3 lb in total
30 ml/2 tbsp plain (all-purpose) flour
Salt and freshly ground black pepper
30 ml/2 tbsp sunflower oil
2 onions, thinly sliced
750 ml/1¼ pts/3 cups beef stock
150 ml/¼ pt/⅔ cup brown ale
10 ml/2 tsp tomato purée (paste)
2 bay leaves
225 g/8 oz small carrots, halved
225 g/8 oz parsnips, cut into large chunks
30 ml/2 tbsp chopped fresh parsley, to garnish

1 Trim the oxtails and cut into large pieces. Season the flour with salt and pepper, then use to coat the meat.

2 Heat the oil in a large, flameproof casserole (Dutch oven) and fry (sauté) the oxtail a few pieces at a time until well browned all over. Remove to a plate and set aside.

3 Add the onions to the casserole and gently fry for 10 minutes until softened and just beginning to brown. Return the meat the dish, then pour in the stock and ale and stir in the tomato purée and bay leaves.

4 Cover and simmer over a very low heat for 2½ hours. Skim off any fat, then stir in the carrots and parsnips.

5 Re-cover and simmer for a further 30 minutes or until tender. Skim again, then remove the bay leaves.

6 Season generously and stir in the parsley.

🕐 **Preparation and cooking time:** 3 hours

Tripe in Creamy Sauce

Although often associated with the north of England, tripe is also popular in the East End. Here, chopped gherkins (cornichons) added to the sauce give it extra flavour.

SERVES 4

450 g/1 lb prepared tripe
2 onions, sliced
600 ml/1 pt/2½ cups milk
1 bay leaf
A pinch of freshly grated nutmeg
Salt and freshly ground black pepper
25 g/1 oz/2 tbsp butter or margarine
15 g/½ oz/1 tbsp plain (all-purpose) flour
6 medium gherkins, finely chopped

1 Cover the tripe with cold water in a pan. Cover, bring to the boil, then drain and rinse. Cut into 2.5 cm/1 in pieces.

2 Return the tripe to the pan with the onions, milk, bay leaf, nutmeg, salt and pepper. Bring to the boil, then reduce the heat, cover and simmer very gently for 2 hours. Strain, reserving the milk and onions and discarding the bay leaf.

3 Melt the butter or margarine in the saucepan. Stir in the flour and cook for 1 minute. Remove from the heat, gradually whisk in the milk, then return to the heat and simmer for a minute until thickened.

4 Return the tripe and onions to the sauce with the gherkins and gently simmer for 2–3 minutes. Season and serve.

⏲ **Preparation and cooking time:** 2¼ hours

> *Trotty … dodged about, from tripe to hot potato, and from hot potato back again to tripe, with an unctuous and unflagging relish.*
> Charles Dickens, *The Chimes*

Bacon Fraize

This economical bacon and batter dish dates back to the fifteenth century and is also known as a 'froise'.

SERVES 2–3

15 ml/1 tbsp sunflower oil
4 thick rashers (slices) of smoked streaky bacon, rinded and
  chopped
50 g/2 oz/½ cup plain (all-purpose) flour
1 whole egg
150 ml/¼ pt/⅔ cup milk
Freshly ground black pepper
1 egg white

1 Heat 5 ml/1 tsp of the oil in a heavy, preferably non-stick, 20 cm/8 in frying pan (skillet). Add the bacon and cook for 3–4 minutes until browned and crispy. Remove and set aside.

2 Meanwhile, sift the flour into a bowl and make a well in the middle. Add the whole egg, the milk and pepper and gradually beat to a thick batter. Whisk the egg white, then fold into the batter, half at a time.

3 Heat the remaining 10 ml/2 tsp of oil in the pan. Pour in the batter, then scatter with the bacon.

4 Cook over a moderate heat until the base is lightly browned and the top just set. Carefully turn over and cook the other side until browned. Cut into wedges and serve straight away.

⏱ **Preparation and cooking time:** 20 minutes

Crispy Pigs' Tails

SERVES 4

4 long pig's tails
1 small onion, roughly chopped
1 carrot, roughly chopped
1 celery stick, sliced
1 bay leaf
2 large sprigs of parsley
6 black peppercorns
600 ml/1 pt/2½ cups pork or vegetable stock
1 egg
2.5 ml/½ tsp made English mustard
60 ml/4 tbsp plain (all-purpose) flour
Salt and freshly ground black pepper
100 g/4 oz/2 cups fine fresh white breadcrumbs
30 ml/2 tbsp sunflower oil
15 g/½ oz/1 tbsp butter or margarine
A little malt vinegar (optional)

1 Wash the pigs' tails and put them in an ovenproof dish with the onion, carrot, celery, bay leaf, parsley and peppercorns. Pour over the stock.

2 Cover the dish with foil and bake at 180°C/350°F/gas mark 4 for 2 hours or until very tender. Remove the tails from the stock and leave them until cool enough to handle. Strain the stock into a bowl.

3 Lightly beat the egg with the mustard. Season the flour with a little salt and pepper. Dust the pigs' tails with the flour, then roll them in the egg and mustard, then in breadcrumbs.

4 Turn up the oven to 200°C/400°F/gas mark 6. Put the oil and butter or margarine in a roasting tin (pan) and heat in the oven for 5 minutes.

5 Add the pigs' tails to the tin and roast for
15–20 minutes, turning once, until they are well browned and
crisp. Serve hot, sprinkled with malt vinegar if liked.

🕑 **Preparation and cooking time:** 2½ hours

➤ **Cook's tip**
Strain the stock, then cool and chill. It will set to a rich jelly,
which can be used as a stock for a casserole or soup.

Brawn

*This is another dish with the gelatinous texture so much enjoyed by
cockneys. If you're going to make it yourself, ask your butcher to
help by halving the head for you.*

SERVES 6
1 pig's head
5 ml/1 tsp salt
1 onion, sliced
1 carrot, roughly chopped
4 large sprigs of parsley
1 bay leaf
6 black peppercorns

1 Put the two halves of the head in a saucepan with all
the other ingredients. Pour in just enough water to cover,
then bring to the boil, cover and simmer for 2 hours or until
the flesh easily comes away from the bones. Leave to cool.

2 When cool enough to handle, remove the head,
reserving the stock, and take off all the meat, including the
tongue. Roughly chop and put into a pudding basin.

3 Return the bones to the stock and simmer, uncovered,
for about 10 minutes until slightly reduced. Strain over the
meat and leave to cool. Chill in the fridge until ready to
serve.

🕑 **Preparation and cooking time:** 2½ hours plus chilling

Pigs' Trotters

Cockneys have always loved all kinds of jellied meats. Pigs' trotters were very much a part of London's street-eating in the eighteenth century and were often eaten by the poor as they were cheap and nourishing. They now frequently feature as a delicacy on the menu of the most expensive restaurants, brushed with melted butter, coated in breadcrumbs, then grilled (broiled) until crisp, or boned and filled with an exquisite stuffing. Traditionally, however, the cooking is kept simple; they're baked and eaten cold, seasoned generously with salt, pepper and vinegar.

SERVES 4

4 pigs' trotters
1 onion, sliced
1 carrot, roughly chopped
2 large sprigs of parsley
2 bay leaves
2.5 ml/½ tsp salt
6 black peppercorns

1 Rinse the trotters and put in a saucepan in which they just fit with the onion, carrot, parsley, bay leaves, salt and peppercorns. Pour in just enough water to cover the trotters.

2 Slowly bring to the boil, then reduce the heat, cover with a lid and simmer for 2–3 hours or until very tender when pierced with a sharp knife or skewer.

3 Remove the trotters and place in a serving dish. Strain over the liquid and leave until cool. Chill until ready to serve – the cooking liquor will set to a well-flavoured jelly, which should be served with the trotters.

⊕ **Preparation and cooking time:** 2–3 hours

➤ **Cook's tip**
Cows' heels can be prepared in exactly the same way; buy them from the butcher, ready-cleaned and split.

Mangsho Jhol

There has been a huge influx of Asians into the East End, particularly Bangladeshis, and along Brick Lane you will find some of the best curry restaurants and Indian food stores in Britain. This classic Bangladeshi dish is delicious served with boiled rice or warm naan bread. Ghee is clarified butter, much used in Indian cookery.

SERVES 6

750 g/1¾ lb lean boned shoulder or leg of lamb, cut into cubes
5 ml/1 tsp ground turmeric
5 ml/1 tsp ground coriander (cilantro)
45 ml/3 tbsp ghee or sunflower oil
2 onions, sliced
5 ml/1 tsp cumin seeds
2 garlic cloves, crushed
2.5 cm/1 in piece of fresh root ginger, peeled and grated
300 ml/½ pt/1¼ cups lamb or vegetable stock
450 g/1 lb waxy potatoes, peeled and cut into chunks
2.5 ml/½ tsp garam masala
30 ml/2 tbsp chopped fresh coriander
Salt, to taste

1 Toss the lamb with the turmeric and coriander, cover and marinate in the fridge for at least 2–3 hours.

2 Heat 30 ml/2 tbsp of the ghee or oil in a large saucepan and gently cook the onions for 10 minutes until beginning to colour.

3 Add the cumin seeds, garlic and ginger and cook, stirring all the time, for 2–3 minutes. Remove and set aside.

4 Heat the remaining ghee or oil and fry (sauté) the meat in two batches until browned all over. Return the onions to the pan and pour in the stock. Gently simmer for 30 minutes.

5 Add the potatoes and simmer for 45 minutes or until the lamb and potatoes are very tender. Stir in the garam masala, chopped coriander and salt to taste. Serve hot.

⏲ **Preparation and cooking time:** 1¾ hours plus marinating

Seafood

illingsgate fish market was moved to the Isle of Dogs in January 1982. You'll no longer see fish-filled baskets skilfully balanced and carried on heads as modern equipment has been introduced, but you can still hear the cockney banter from the friendly market porters. The original 900-year-old market was situated between London Bridge and the Tower of London and once sold other foods including fruit and salt as well as fish. The new market is open to the public although you may have to buy in bulk. You'll also have to be an early riser, however, as trade finishes by about 8.30 am!

Cockneys, it must be said, have never eaten a great range of fish. However, smoked and salted fish, such as kippers served with thickly sliced bread, and battered skate from the fish and chip shop were great favourites with the East Enders who also enjoyed jellied eels, cockles and winkles from street traders.

Please remember the grotto,
It's only once a year.
My father's gone to sea,
My mother's gone to fetch him back,
So please remember me.
Children's chant

Baked Oysters

*The symbol of James, one of Christ's disciples, was an oyster shell.
On St James' Day, which falls on 25 July, London children used to
build small grottoes from oyster shells (and later when shells were
more difficult to get, from pebbles and flowers) and chant a little
rhyme to collect pennies from passers-by.*

SERVES 3–4

12 large oysters
100 ml/3½ fl oz/scant ½ cup double (heavy) cream
30 ml/2 tbsp chopped fresh parsley
Salt and freshly ground black pepper
*50 g/2 oz/½ cup Gruyère (Swiss) or Cheddar cheese, finely
    grated*
30 ml/2 tbsp fresh white breadcrumbs

1 Preheat the oven to 200°C/400°F/gas mark 6. Put the
oysters on a baking (cookie) sheet with the flat sides
uppermost.

2 Bake in the oven for 3–4 minutes or until the shells
open. When cool enough to handle, remove the upper shells,
taking care to keep in the juices.

3 Mix the cream and parsley together with a little salt
and pepper. Spoon the mixture over each oyster.

4 Mix the cheese and breadcrumbs and sprinkle over the
top. Return to the oven for 5 minutes or until the tops are
crisp and golden.

⊕ **Preparation and cooking time:** 15 minutes

➤ **Cook's tip**
To make sure that the oysters don't tip over and lose their
precious juices, put them in the individual sections of a bun
tin (patty pan).

Traditional Fish and Chips

Chips (fries) are a perennial favourite in most homes and the East End still has some of the finest fish and chip shops – 'chippies' – in the country. Unlike the skinny, chemically seasoned French fries many of us are now used to, the traditional chip-shop chip is thickly cut and cooked in lard (shortening), so that it is crisp on the outside and meltingly soft in the middle. I prefer to use oil for cooking, however. Corn oil is ideal as it has a very high smoking point; otherwise use sunflower, safflower or groundnut oil.

SERVES 4

4 cod or haddock fillets, about 175 g/6 oz each, skinned
50 g/2 oz/½ cup plain (all-purpose) flour
100 g/4 oz/1 cup self-raising (self-rising) flour
2.5 ml/½ tsp salt
200 ml/7 fl oz/scant 1 cup cold water
Oil, for deep-frying
4 large potatoes

1 Pat the fish dry on kitchen paper (paper towels), then lightly dust with the plain flour.

2 Sift the self-raising flour and salt into a large bowl. Make a well in the middle and add the water. Gradually mix the flour into the liquid and beat until smooth.

3 Half-fill a deep frying pan (skillet) with oil and heat to 190°C/375°F, or until a cube of day-old bread browns in 30 seconds. Dip each piece of fish into the batter, then cook two pieces at a time for 5–6 minutes or until golden brown and crisp.

4 Drain on kitchen paper and keep hot while you cook the second batch.

5 For the chips, cut the potatoes into thick slices, then cut across into thick fingers. Leave in a bowl of cold water for 20 minutes to remove excess starch. Drain and dry on kitchen paper or on a clean tea towel (dish cloth).

6 Half-fill a deep frying pan or electric deep-fat fryer with oil and heat to 190°C/375°F or until a chip dropped in rises to the surface straight away surrounded by bubbles. Quarter-fill a frying basket with potato chips, lower into the hot oil and cook for 6 minutes. Remove and drain. Repeat with the remaining chips.

7 Bring the oil back up to temperature, then cook all the chips together for a second time for about 3 minutes just until crisp and golden. Drain and serve with the fish.

🕐 **Preparation and cooking time:** 20 minutes

➤ **Cook's tip**
You can use up potato peelings to make Crispy Potato Skins. Make sure you have peeled the potatoes thickly. Pat the peelings dry, then fry (sauté) in oil heated to 180°C/350°F for 3 minutes. Drain and allow the oil to come back up to temperature, then fry for 2 further minutes until crisp.

Buttered Bloaters

Bloaters are fresh herrings, gutted but not split, then lightly salted and delicately smoked. They were extremely popular in Victorian times, especially for high tea. Although now more difficult to find in the East End, some are still brought in from Great Yarmouth.

SERVES 4
4 bloaters or other smoked fish
25 g/1 oz/2 tbsp unsalted (sweet) butter
Freshly ground black pepper

1 Preheat the grill (broiler) until hot. Cut the head and tail off each bloater, open it down its back and spread it flat. Make three or four shallow slashes on each side.

2 Dot the bloaters with butter and grill (broil) for 4–5 minutes on each side until blistered. Serve hot.

🕐 **Preparation and cooking time:** 10 minutes

Sizzling Sprats

Caught in large quantities off the east coast of England, these fish are very popular on the cockney market stalls and are available between October and March. Buy small ones for this dish; if they're more than 5 cm/2 in long, they should be gutted and boned before cooking, but the little ones can be eaten whole, as here.

SERVES 2

225 g/8 oz small sprats
60 ml/4 tbsp plain (all-purpose) flour
Salt and freshly ground pepper
25 g/1 oz/2 tbsp butter or margarine
30 ml/2 tbsp vegetable oil
15 ml/1 tbsp lemon juice

1 Pat the sprats dry on kitchen paper (paper towels). Put in a large bowl and sprinkle over the flour, salt and pepper. Gently toss the sprats to coat in the seasoned flour.

2 Heat the butter or margarine and oil in a large frying pan (skillet). When it is smoking hot, tip in the sprats.

3 Turn down the heat to medium-high and fry (sauté) for about 5 minutes until crisp and brown, shaking the pan frequently for even cooking. Sprinkle with lemon juice and serve straight away.

⏲ **Preparation and cooking time:** 20 minutes

Smoked Haddock Fishcakes

Fish cakes are an economical way of making fish go further and when times were hard, the proportion of potato to smoked haddock would be increased. Coating with breadcrumbs is a more modern treatment; if preferred, you can simply dust the outsides with flour.

SERVES 4

400 g/14 oz smoked haddock, preferably undyed
400 g/14 oz potatoes, cut into large chunks
Salt and freshly ground pepper
25 g/1 oz/2 tbsp butter or margarine
6 spring onions (scallions), trimmed and finely chopped
15 ml/1 tbsp snipped fresh chives
1 egg, lightly beaten
50 g/2 oz/½ cup fresh white breadcrumbs
30 ml/2 tbsp oil, for shallow-frying

1 Put the haddock in a saucepan and pour in enough cold water to cover. Bring to the boil, then reduce the heat, cover and simmer for 10–12 minutes or until the fish is just cooked and still slightly opaque. Remove and flake the fish, discarding the skin and any bones.

2 Cook the potatoes in boiling water for 15 minutes or until tender. Drain thoroughly and mash until smooth. Season to taste with salt and pepper.

3 Melt the butter or margarine in a frying pan (skillet) and gently fry (sauté) the spring onions for 4–5 minutes until soft. Stir into the mashed potato with the fish, chives and 15 ml/1 tbsp of the beaten egg.

4 With floured hands, shape the mixture into eight round fish cakes, about 2 cm/¾ in thick. Dip in the remaining beaten egg, then in breadcrumbs to coat. Chill in the fridge for 30 minutes to firm.

5 Heat the oil in a heavy frying pan and fry over a medium heat for 5–6 minutes on each side until golden brown. Serve hot.

⊕ **Preparation and cooking time:** 45 minutes plus chilling

Smoky Fish Pie

SERVES 6

4 rashers (slices) of smoked streaky bacon, rinded and chopped
450 g/1 lb smoked haddock or cod fillet
1 bay leaf
1 small onion, sliced
400 ml/14 fl oz/1¾ cups milk
50 g/2 oz/¼ cup butter or margarine
45 ml/3 tbsp plain (all-purpose) flour
2 eggs, hard-boiled (hard-cooked) and chopped
45 ml/3 tbsp chopped fresh parsley
750 g/1¾ lb potatoes
Salt and freshly ground black pepper

1 Dry-fry the bacon in a saucepan for 3–4 minutes until lightly browned. Remove from the pan and set aside. Put the fish, bay leaf and onion in the saucepan. Reserve 60 ml/ 4 tbsp of the milk and pour the rest over the fish.

2 Slowly bring to the boil, then reduce the heat, cover and simmer for 7–8 minutes or until the fish is only half-cooked. Remove from the milk with a slotted spoon and flake, removing the skin and any bones. Strain the milk, reserving the bay leaf and rinse out the pan.

3 Melt 40 g/1½ oz/3 tbsp of the butter or margarine in the pan. Stir in the flour and cook for a few seconds, then remove from the heat. Gradually whisk in the strained milk and add the bay leaf. Simmer for 2–3 minutes until smooth and thick, stirring all the time. Remove the bay leaf.

4 Stir the fish into the sauce with the chopped eggs, parsley and pepper to taste. Spoon into a 1.2 litre/2 pt/5 cup ovenproof dish.

5 Meanwhile, cook the potatoes in boiling salted water for 15 minutes or until tender. Drain and mash with the remaining 15 g/½ oz/1 tbsp butter or margarine, the reserved milk and some black pepper to taste.

6 Spoon or pipe on top of the fish mixture and place the dish on a baking (cookie) tray. Bake in a preheated oven at 200°C/400°F/gas mark 6 for 25 minutes or until the potato is golden brown.

⊕ **Preparation and cooking time:** 1 hour

➤ **Cook's tip**
Serve this with any green vegetable of your choice.

Jellied Eels

This is perhaps the most famous dish of the East End and little bowls of jellied eels and seafood are still sold at stalls outside pubs throughout London. The eel should be as fresh as possible.

SERVES 4
1 large fresh eel, skinned if preferred
1 bay leaf
A sprig of thyme
4 black peppercorns
15 ml/1 tbsp white wine vinegar
Salt and freshly ground black pepper

1 Cut the eel into 2.5 cm/1 in pieces and put in a saucepan with the bay leaf, thyme and peppercorns. Pour in just enough water to cover the fish.

2 Slowly bring to the boil, then reduce the heat, cover and simmer for 35–50 minutes, depending on the thickness of the eel, until very tender when pierced with a fine knife or skewer.

3 Transfer the pieces of eel to a bowl. Stir the vinegar into the liquid in the pan, then strain over the eel, discarding the bay leaf, thyme and peppercorns.

4 Leave to cool, then chill in the fridge. The liquid will become a lightly set, clear jelly.

⊕ **Preparation and cooking time:** 1 hour plus chilling

Eel Pie

Traditionally, eels should be freshly killed immediately before cooking. This is not really feasible for most of us, but it is worth trying to buy them as fresh as possible from a fish market, if you can.

SERVES 4

100 g/4 oz/1 cup plain (all-purpose) flour
Salt
50 g/2 oz/¼ cup butter or half butter, half white fat
30 ml/2 tbsp cold water
For the filling:
2 large cooking (tart) apples
30 ml/2 tbsp apple juice or water
15 g/½ oz/1 tbsp butter or margarine, softened
1 garlic clove, crushed
450 g/1 lb fresh eel, cut into 2.5 cm/1 in pieces
15 ml/1 tbsp malt vinegar
A pinch of ground mace
Freshly ground black pepper
Beaten egg or milk, to glaze

1 Sift the flour and a pinch of salt into a mixing bowl. Add the fat and rub in until the mixture resembles breadcrumbs. Sprinkle over the water and mix to a firm dough. Wrap in clingfilm (plastic wrap) and chill in the fridge for 20 minutes.

2 Meanwhile, prepare the filling for the pie. Quarter, core and peel the apples. Roughly chop and put in a saucepan with the apple juice or water. Cover and simmer for 15 minutes until soft. Mash to a purée and leave to cool.

3 Blend the butter or margarine and garlic together and use to grease a pie dish. Toss the eel in the vinegar, then sprinkle with a little mace, salt and pepper and put into the dish. Spoon the apple purée between the gaps.

4 Roll out the pastry (paste) on a lightly floured surface until 5 cm/2 in larger than the dish. Cut off a 2.5 cm/1 in strip from around the edge. Moisten the rim of the pie dish and position the strip on the rim, then brush with water.

5 Lift the pastry lid into position. Press the edges together to seal. Trim off the excess pastry, knock up the edges with the blunt edge of a knife, then flute or press with the back of a floured fork around the edge to make a pattern.

6 Brush the pastry with beaten egg or milk to glaze, then make a couple of steam-holes in the top. Place on a baking (cookie) tray and bake at 200°C/400°F/gas mark 6 for 30 minutes until golden brown. Serve hot or leave to cool, when the filling will have set to a soft jelly.

🕐 **Preparation and cooking time:** 1 hour plus chilling

Devilled Coley

Coley is a relatively inexpensive fish, but any white fish may be used.

SERVES 4

4 coley fillets, about 150 g/5 oz each
30 ml/2 tbsp plain (all-purpose) flour
Salt and freshly ground pepper
25 g/1 oz/2 tbsp butter or margarine
15 ml/1 tbsp Worcestershire sauce
5 ml/1 tsp made English mustard
15 ml/1 tbsp mango chutney
15 ml/1 tbsp orange juice

1 Pat the fish fillets dry on kitchen paper (paper towels), then sprinkle with the flour, seasoned with salt and pepper.

2 Heat the butter or margarine in a frying pan (skillet) until sizzling, add the fish and fry (sauté) for 3–4 minutes on each side until firm. Remove from the pan and keep warm.

3 Add all the remaining ingredients to the pan and heat, stirring, until bubbling. Drizzle over the fish and serve.

🕐 **Preparation and cooking time:** 15 minutes

Crispy Whitebait

Whitebait are young sprats and herrings about the length of your little finger. They're always eaten whole, floured or battered, then deep-fried.

SERVES 4

75 g/3 oz/¾ cup plain (all-purpose) flour
2.5 ml/½ tsp salt
150 ml/¼ pint/⅔ cup dry cider
15 g/½ oz/1 tbsp butter or margarine, melted
450 g/1 lb whitebait
Oil, for deep-frying
Wedges of lemon and brown bread and butter, to serve

1 Sift the flour and salt into a bowl and make a well in the middle. Pour in the cider and butter or margarine, then mix to a smooth batter, gradually drawing in the flour.

2 Rinse the whitebait and pat dry on kitchen paper (paper towels). Half-fill a deep-fat fryer with oil and heat to 180°C/350°F, or until a cube of day-old bread browns in 30 seconds.

3 Divide the fish into four batches. Dip each batch in the batter, then cook for 3–4 minutes until golden brown and crisp. Drain on kitchen paper and keep warm.

4 Bring the oil back up to the correct temperature before cooking the next batch. Serve hot with wedges of lemon and brown bread and butter.

⏲ **Preparation and cooking time:** 20 minutes

Grilled Kippers

Kippers are herrings that have been split down the middle, gutted, salted and smoked, usually over oak. Cheap and easy to prepare, their popularity was partly due to the fact that they kept well in the days before refrigeration. Serve them with bread and butter and mugs of strong tea, for a simple but satisfying lunch or supper. East End traders still refer to days when business is flat as 'kipper days', but be wary of the cockney who calls you a 'kipper'; this isn't a term of endearment – it means you have no guts!

SERVES 4

4 kippers
Freshly ground black pepper
A little malt vinegar or lemon juice

1 Preheat the grill (broiler) until hot. Line the grill pan with foil and place the kippers in it, skin-side up.

2 Grill (broil) for 3–4 minutes or until the skins are browned and crisp, then turn over and grill for a further 3–4 minutes until piping hot.

3 Serve sprinkled with vinegar or lemon juice.

🕐 **Preparation and cooking time:** 10 minutes

➤ **Cook's tip**
Jugged Kippers are also popular and simple to prepare. Place the kippers tail-ends-up in a large jug and pour in enough boiling water to cover. Leave for 4–5 minutes, by which time the kippers will be piping hot. Drain well before serving. This method keeps the flesh moist and lessens the smoky, salty flavour.

Balti Bengali Fish

The East End now has a large population of Bangladeshis (from West Bengal) who have influenced the cuisine of the area. Hundreds of varieties of fresh fish are available from local Billingsgate market and are used to make curries such as this one. Jaggery is unrefined brown sugar, available in ethnic stores.

SERVES 4

30 ml/2 tbsp ghee or vegetable oil
1 large onion, chopped
3 garlic cloves, finely chopped
2 red chillies, seeded and finely chopped
30 ml/2 tbsp masala curry paste
4 ripe tomatoes, skinned, seeded and chopped
150 ml/¼ pt/⅔ cup fish or vegetable stock
10 ml/2 tsp jaggery or soft light brown sugar
700 g/1½ lb whole fillet of firm fish, such as cod
225 g/8 oz cooked waxy potatoes, cubed
150 ml/¼ pt/⅔ cup plain Greek-style yoghurt
10 ml/2 tsp garam masala
30 ml/2 tbsp chopped fresh coriander (cilantro)
Salt and freshly ground black pepper

1 Heat the ghee or oil in a large, heavy-based frying pan (skillet) and gently cook the onion for 10 minutes until soft. Stir in the garlic, chillies and curry paste and cook for 2 more minutes, stirring all the time.

2 Add the tomatoes, stock and jaggery or sugar. Stir well, then place the fish on top. Spoon some of the juices over the fish, then cover and simmer gently for 12 minutes or until the fish is opaque and cooked through.

3 Transfer the fish to a warmed serving dish, cover and keep warm. Add the potatoes to the pan and cook over a high heat until bubbling fiercely.

4 Turn down the heat to very low. Stir a spoonful of the sauce into the yoghurt, then add the yoghurt to the pan with the garam masala and half the coriander. Season to taste.

5 Heat for a few minutes, but do not allow to boil or it may curdle. Spoon the sauce over the fish and serve sprinkled with the remaining coriander.

🕐 **Preparation and cooking time:** 40 minutes

➤ **Cook's tip**
Potatoes are the classic addition to this dish, but you can serve it with rice or naan bread, if liked.

Oatmeal-crusted Herrings

During Victorian times, the average Londoner ate 7 kg/16 lb of herrings in a year! They have remained popular in the East End, although perhaps in not quite the same quantities.

SERVES 4
4 herrings, about 225 g/8 oz each, filleted
15 ml/1 tbsp sunflower oil
10 ml/2 tsp lemon juice
Salt and freshly ground pepper
60 ml/4 tbsp pinhead oatmeal
Finely grated rind of ½ lemon
Wedges of lemon, to serve

1 Rinse the herring fillets and pat dry on kitchen paper (paper towels). Mix the oil and lemon juice and brush over the fleshy side of each. Season with salt and pepper.

2 Line the grill (broiler) pan with foil and place the fillets, flesh-side up, on the rack in a single layer.

3 Mix the oatmeal and lemon rind together and sprinkle evenly over the fish, then press down lightly.

4 Cook under a medium-hot grill for about 5 minutes, without turning the fish, until they are cooked through. Serve hot with wedges of lemon to squeeze over.

🕐 **Preparation and cooking time:** 10 minutes

Cockles, Winkles, Whelks and Mussels

Years ago, during the summer months a train known as 'the cockle special' would stop at every station in the East End on its way to Southend, the closest seaside resort to the East End, and therefore the cockneys' favourite. Families would spend a day walking out along the muddy sands of the outgoing tide, looking for tell-tale air-holes where cockles would be buried just below the surface, or gathering winkles from the rock pools. The shrimp and winkle man would tour the streets at the weekend, crying 'Shrimps and winkles, all fresh today', and shellfish was always a part of a traditional Sunday tea, usually eaten from the shells with a pin.

➤ Cockles, Winkles and Whelks

These are usually sold cooked and shelled, then tossed in vinegar. To prepare fresh, wash thoroughly in plenty of cold water, discarding any that won't shut tightly when tapped, then soak in cold water for 2 hours. Steam or cook in a small amount of water for about 5 minutes for cockles and winkles or 15 for whelks. Discard any cockles that remain closed. Remove the cockles from their shells, then cook for a further 2–3 minutes. Extract winkles and whelks from the shells with a long pin. Serve with vinegar or lemon juice and pepper and thin slices of bread and butter.

🕐 **Preparation and cooking time:** 20 minutes plus soaking

➤ Mussels

These are sold either by volume or by weight: 1.2 litres/ 2 pts/1 quart/5 cups of mussels is the equivalent of 900 g/ 2 lb. To prepare fresh mussels, rinse under cold, running water, then scrub the shells to remove any barnacles and pull off the hairy 'beards' protruding from the shells. Tap any open ones sharply with a knife and throw away if they do not close. Put in a saucepan with a wineglass of white wine or cider, a knob of butter and a crushed clove or two of garlic, if liked. Cover tightly and steam for 4–5 minutes or until opened, shaking the pan now and then. Discard any that remain shut.

🕐 **Preparation and cooking time:** 20 minutes

East End Kosher

The Jews who fled from Eastern Europe, although poor and with few possessions, brought a vast culinary knowledge with them. Many travelled by the cheapest means – cattle boats, which landed in the docks at the East End of London – and because they had insufficient money to travel elsewhere, they settled in the area. Soon there were Jewish shops, schools and synagogues throughout the East End. Few were truly integrated into the tight-knit cockney community, but their influence on the local cuisine was strong and some restaurants, such as Blooms of Whitechapel, gained a worldwide reputation for their kosher food. As the Jews prospered through hard work, many moved from the area into more affluent parts of the country and the East End Jewish population slowly dwindled. Blooms closed in 1996, but many Jewish grocers and bakeries remain.

Latkes

These potato pancakes are usually served as an accompaniment to the main meal with apple sauce, but small ones make a good appetiser, topped with soured (dairy sour) cream and lumpfish roe or caviar. Schmaltz is rendered chicken fat, frequently used in Jewish cooking to add a unique flavour (see Cook's tip, below).

SERVES 6

6 waxy potatoes
1 small onion, finely grated
2 eggs, lightly beaten
75 g/3 oz/¾ cup matzo meal or plain (all-purpose) flour
Salt and freshly ground black pepper
60 ml/4 tbsp schmaltz or sunflower oil

1 Coarsely grate the potatoes and squeeze out as much liquid as possible. Put in a mixing bowl with the onion, eggs, matzo meal or flour and salt and pepper. Mix together thoroughly.

2 Heat half the schmaltz or oil in a large heavy-based frying pan (skillet). Add large tablespoonfuls of the potato mixture and flatten into rounds.

3 Fry (sauté) for about 6 minutes until crisp and golden brown, then turn over and cook the other sides. Keep warm in a low oven while cooking the remaining cakes, adding more fat to the pan as necessary. Serve hot.

⊕ **Preparation and cooking time:** 20 minutes

➤ **Cook's tip**
To make schmaltz, remove the excess fat every time you prepare a chicken and store in the freezer until you have at least 225 g/8 oz/1 cup. Place it in a heavy-based saucepan with just enough water to cover, add a small, chopped onion, cover the pan and simmer for 15 minutes. Uncover and cook until the water has evaporated. Strain to remove the onion and when cool, store in the fridge or freezer.

Chicken Soup

*Home-made chicken soup is very much a part of basic Jewish
cooking, often served when someone is unwell because of its
comforting and perceived healing properties. The recipe can be
varied depending on what vegetables are available, and other
grains, such as rice, or pasta, can be added instead of the barley.*

SERVES 6
15 ml/1 tbsp sunflower oil
1 onion, finely chopped
2 carrots, chopped
2 celery sticks, chopped
1 garlic clove, crushed
2 large sprigs of parsley
1.5 kg/3 lb chicken, quartered and skinned
15 g/½ oz pearl barley, rinsed
Salt and freshly ground black pepper
1.2 litres/2 pts/5 cups good-quality chicken stock
Chopped fresh parsley, to garnish

1 Heat the oil in a saucepan, and cook the onion over a
low heat for 10 minutes until soft but not coloured.

2 Add the carrots, celery and garlic and cook for a few
more minutes, stirring all the time, then add the parsley,
chicken portions, barley, salt and pepper.

3 Pour over the stock; it should cover the chicken and
vegetables. If not, add a little more stock or water.

4 Bring to the boil, then lower the heat and simmer for
50 minutes or until the chicken and the barley are tender.
Remove the chicken and leave until cool enough to handle.

5 Remove and discard the chicken bones and dice the
meat. Skim any fat from the surface of the soup and remove
the parsley. Stir in the diced chicken and reheat.

6 Ladle into warmed bowls and sprinkle with parsley.

⏱ **Preparation and cooking time:** 1¼ hours

Gefilte Fish

*These poached fish balls are usually served as a first course
accompanied by horseradish sauce.*

SERVES 4

15 ml/1 tbsp oil
1 small onion, very finely chopped
450 g/1 lb white fish fillets, such as carp or pike
75 g/3 oz/1½ cups fine slightly dry white breadcrumbs
2 eggs
A pinch of freshly grated nutmeg
Salt and freshly ground black pepper
750 ml/1¼ pts/3 cups fish stock (see Cook's tip, opposite)

1 Heat the oil in a small pan, add the onion and cook
over a low heat for 7–8 minutes until softened, but not
coloured. Leave to cool.

2 Remove the skin and any bones from the fish and cut it
into small cubes. Put it in a food processor with the onion,
breadcrumbs, eggs, nutmeg, salt and pepper and purée until
smooth. Remove and chill the mixture for at least 1 hour.

3 Shape heaped teaspoonfuls of the fish mixture into
small balls or ovals. Place on a plate and chill again to firm
them, so that they hold their shape when cooked.

4 Bring the fish stock to the boil in a wide, shallow pan,
then turn down the heat to a gentle simmer. Add the fish
balls and poach for 10 minutes, turning them halfway
through. Remove with a slotted spoon and set aside to cool.

5 Turn up the heat a little and boil the fish stock for
about 10 minutes to reduce slightly. Allow to cool, then chill
until set to a jelly. Remove any fat from the top and serve the
jellied sauce with the fish balls.

☺ **Preparation and cooking time:** 45 minutes plus chilling

➤ **Cook's tip**

For the fish stock, rinse 900 g/2 lb fish bones and trimmings and put in a large saucepan with 1 chopped onion, 2 sliced carrots, 2 sliced celery sticks, 1 bay leaf, 6 white peppercorns and 2.5 ml/½ tsp sea salt. Pour in 900 ml/1½ pts/3¾ cups cold water. Slowly bring to the boil and skim. Simmer gently for 30 minutes. Strain through a fine sieve (strainer), cool quickly, cover and chill. Use within two days.

Schmaltz Herrings

Even at the turn of the twentieth century, rickets was a common disease, especially among the poor, due to lack of calcium and vitamin D in the diet. Jewish children in the East End rarely suffered from this crippling disease, however, because their immigrant parents had brought with them a taste for fresh, pickled and salted herrings, which provided these essential nutrients.

SERVES 4

8 pickled rollmop herrings, drained
2 eating (dessert) apples, peeled, cored and thinly sliced
15 ml/1 tbsp lemon juice
1 small onion, very thinly sliced
150 ml/¼ pt/⅔ cup soured (dairy sour) cream
6 gherkins (cornichons), very finely chopped
Salt and freshly ground black pepper
A pinch of cayenne pepper
10 ml/2 tsp chopped fresh parsley

1 Slice the herrings and arrange in a shallow serving dish. Toss the apple slices in the lemon juice to prevent them from browning, then arrange on top with the onion slices.

2 Mix the soured cream with the gherkins and a little salt and pepper. Drizzle over the fish, apples and onions.

3 Sprinkle with a little cayenne pepper and chopped parsley and serve immediately.

🕐 **Preparation time:** 15 minutes

Chicken Liver Pâté

This favourite dish is delicious spread generously on crackers, small matzos or thinly sliced rye bread.

SERVES 6

50 g/2 oz/¼ cup margarine or schmaltz (see page 54)
1 small onion, finely chopped
2 garlic cloves, crushed
450 g/1 lb chicken livers, trimmed and roughly chopped
15 ml/1 tbsp sweet sherry or Madeira
Salt and freshly ground black pepper
30 ml/2 tbsp chopped fresh parsley

1 Melt 20 g/¾ oz/4 tsp of the margarine or schmaltz in a frying pan (skillet), add the onion and gently cook for 10 minutes until soft. Stir in the garlic and cook for 1 more minute. Transfer to a food processor or blender.

2 Melt the remaining margarine or schmaltz in the pan, then add the chicken livers. Cook briskly over a high heat for a few minutes until the livers are browned on the outside, but still a little pink on the inside. Remove from the pan and add to the food processor.

3 Add the sherry or Madeira, salt and pepper and blend for about 1 minute until thoroughly combined, but not completely smooth.

4 Stir in the parsley and adjust the seasoning if necessary. Spoon into a dish, cover and chill for at least 1 hour before serving.

⏀ **Preparation and cooking time:** 25 minutes plus chilling

Challah

%%

This golden egg-enriched bread, whose name means 'offering', is usually made as a plait-shaped loaf for the Jewish Sabbath. The three braids symbolise truth, peace and justice. The dough may also be coiled when served to celebrate the Jewish New Year, Rosh Hashanah.

MAKES 1 LOAF

450 g/1 lb/4 cups strong white plain (bread) flour
2.5 ml/½ tsp salt
10 ml/2 tsp easy-blend dried yeast
2 eggs, lightly beaten
50 g/2 oz/¼ cup butter, melted
200 ml/7 fl oz/scant 1 cup lukewarm water
30 ml/2 tbsp clear honey
1 egg, beaten, to glaze
15 ml/1 tbsp poppy seeds

1 Sift the flour and salt into a large mixing bowl. Stir in the yeast and make a well in the middle.

2 Mix together the eggs, butter, water and honey. Add to the dry ingredients and mix to a soft dough. Knead on a floured surface for 10 minutes until smooth and elastic.

3 Put in a bowl, cover with clingfilm (plastic wrap) and leave in a warm place for 1½ hours or until doubled in size.

4 Knock back (punch down) the dough, then divide into three equal pieces. Roll out each to form a 30 cm/12 in rope, then plait the ropes together, pinching the ends together to seal.

5 Transfer to a greased baking (cookie) sheet, cover with oiled clingfilm and leave to rise for a further 45 minutes, or until doubled in size.

6 Lightly brush with egg to glaze and sprinkle with poppy seeds. Bake in a preheated oven at 180°C/350°F/gas mark 4 for 40–45 minutes or until golden brown and hollow-sounding when tapped underneath. Cool on a wire rack.

⏲ **Preparation and cooking time:** 1¼ hours plus rising

Bagels

Few Eastenders baked their own bread, but Jews who settled in the area soon set up bakeries. One of the best known is 'Beigel Bake' on Brick Lane in Shoreditch. It's open 24 hours a day, seven days a week and is frequented by many celebrities. It sells over 8,000 bagels (or beigels) daily, as well as platzels, which are similar to bagels but without the hole, and a huge range of other breads and cakes. Bagels are briefly dipped in boiling water before baking, which gives them their deliciously chewy crust and soft centre. Traditionally they were made with fresh yeast, but as this is now difficult to find, easy-blend dried yeast has been used here.

MAKES 12
450 g/1 lb/4 cups strong white plain (bread) flour
7.5 ml/1½ tsp salt
10 ml/2 tsp easy-blend dried yeast
3 eggs
5 ml/1 tsp clear honey
15 ml/1 tbsp sunflower oil
250 ml/8 fl oz/1 cup warm water

1 Sift the flour and salt into a mixing bowl, then stir in the yeast. Make a well in the middle. Beat two of the eggs together with the honey and oil. Add to the dry ingredients with the water and mix to a soft dough.

2 Turn out the dough on to a lightly floured surface and knead for about 10 minutes until smooth and elastic. Place in a clean bowl, cover with a tea towel (dish cloth) and leave to rise in a warm place for 45 minutes or until doubled in size.

3 Re-knead the dough and divide into 12 equal pieces. Form each into a roll, 20 cm/8 in long, then dampen the ends, slightly overlap them and squeeze them together to form a ring. Place on an oiled baking (cookie) sheet, cover with oiled clingfilm (plastic wrap) and leave to rise for 20 minutes.

4 Preheat the oven to 200°C/400°F/gas mark 6. Bring a large pan of lightly salted water to the boil. Drop the bagels into the water one at a time and poach for 15 seconds. Lift out with a slotted spoon and return to the baking sheet. Beat the remaining egg and lightly brush over the tops.

5 Bake the bagels for 15 minutes, or until they are well risen and golden brown. Remove from the baking sheet and cool on a wire rack.

🕑 **Preparation and cooking time:** 40 minutes plus rising

➤ **Cook's tip**
For an attractive finish, sprinkle the tops of the bagels with sesame, poppy or caraway seeds after brushing with the egg glaze and before baking. You can also make sweet rather than savoury bagels by adding 30 ml/2 tbsp caster (superfine) sugar, 5 ml/1 tsp ground cinnamon and 50 g/2 oz/⅓ cup raisins to the dry ingredients.

Honey Cake

Many cakes that originated in Eastern Europe contain breadcrumbs and nuts instead of flour, which gives them a wonderfully moist texture and delicious flavour. This cake is traditionally baked in a fluted tin (pan), such as a brioche tin, and is served for Rosh Hashanah, the Jewish New Year. It is best made the day before.

SERVES 10

15 g/½ oz/1 tbsp unsalted (sweet) butter, softened
100 g/4 oz/2 cups day-old fine white breadcrumbs
175 g/6 oz/¾ cup set honey
50 g/2 oz/¼ cup caster (superfine) sugar
2.5 ml/½ tsp ground cinnamon
4 eggs, separated
100 g/4 oz/1 cup finely chopped nuts, such as almonds or
  hazelnuts (filberts)

1 Use the butter to grease a 1.75 litre/3 pt/7½ cup fluted tin. Sprinkle with 15 ml/1 tbsp of the breadcrumbs.

2 Put the honey, sugar and cinnamon in a large mixing bowl set over a pan of gently simmering water and stir until the honey melts. Remove the bowl from the heat.

3 Add the egg yolks and whisk until the mixture is frothy. Fold in the nuts and the remaining breadcrumbs.

4 Whisk the egg whites until stiff. Stir a large spoonful into the mixture to loosen it, then gently fold in the rest.

5 Pour the mixture into the prepared tin and bake in a preheated oven at 180ºC/350ºF/gas mark 4 for 45 minutes or until firm and lightly browned.

6 Leave in the tin for 10 minutes, then turn out and cool on a wire rack. Cut into thick slices to serve.

⏲ **Preparation and cooking time:** 1 hour

Sweet Treats

As fruit came into the London docks, any that was too ripe to be transported out of the city would be sold off cheaply. For the East End families, whose range cookers in the kitchen would be on all day in the winter, this meant that fruit pies and tarts and steamed puddings were everyday fare and as important a part of the meal as the main course.

Costermongers are street traders who sell fruit and vegetables. Their name was derived from a once-common variety of large cooking (tart) apple called a costard. To prevent others from taking their pitches and their trade, the costermongers evolved a system where a leading family would be responsible for protecting the interests of the rest. These families became the Pearly Queens and Kings and one of today's great London sights is the Harvest Festival at the church of St Martin-in-the-Fields in Trafalgar Square, where the costermongers turn out in their wonderful pearl-button-encrusted suits.

Like all children, cockney kids have a sweet tooth. There were once many small sweet factories in the East End where hand-made treats such as humbugs and sticky toffees were made. Sadly they have all disappeared, as have the street sellers with their trays of gingerbread and muffins, but the old traditional recipes have remained and you can still buy these delights in local bakeries.

English Apple Pie

This is an all-time favourite, enjoyed not only in the East End, but also throughout Britain. In the filling, cooking apples are combined with flour, sugar and spices to thicken the juices as the fruit cooks.

SERVES 6

For the pastry (paste):
350 g/12 oz/3 cups plain (all-purpose) flour
A pinch of salt
175 g/6 oz/¾ cup butter, cubed
75 ml/5 tbsp cold water
For the filling:
900 g/2 lb cooking (tart) apples, such as Bramleys, peeled,
  cored and thickly sliced
75 g/3 oz/scant ½ cup caster (superfine) sugar
2.5 ml/½ tsp ground cinnamon
A pinch of ground cloves
45 ml/3 tbsp plain flour
For the glaze:
1 beaten egg or egg white
15 ml/1 tbsp granulated sugar
Custard or whipped cream, to serve

1 Sift the flour and salt into a bowl. Add the butter and rub in until the mixture resembles breadcrumbs. Sprinkle the water over and mix to a firm dough. Lightly knead on a floured surface for a few seconds until smooth, then wrap in clingfilm (plastic wrap) and chill in the fridge for 30 minutes.

2 To make the filling, put the apples in a bowl and sprinkle over the sugar, spices and flour. Gently toss together to coat.

3 Put a heavy baking (cookie) sheet in the oven and preheat to 200°C/400°F/gas mark 6. Roll out slightly more than half of the pastry and use to line a 23 cm/8 in pie dish, about 4 cm/1½ in deep. Spoon in the filling.

4 Brush the pastry edges with a little water, then roll out the remaining pastry to make a lid and place on top of the filling. Gently press the pastry edges together, trim with a sharp knife, then flute, or make a pattern around the edge with the back of a fork. If liked, re-roll the trimmings and cut out leaves to decorate the top of the pie.

5 Brush the top with the beaten egg or egg white and sprinkle with sugar. Make a few steam-holes, then place on the heated baking sheet and cook for 25 minutes. Turn down the oven temperature to 180°C/350°F/gas mark 4 and cook for a further 20 minutes or until the pastry is golden brown.

6 Serve with custard or whipped cream.

⏱ **Preparation and cooking time:** 1 hour plus chilling

➤ **Cook's tip**
This all-butter shortcrust pastry (basic pie crust) gives excellent flavour and colour, but for a shorter texture you can use half lard (shortening) or white vegetable fat.

Cherry Pie

There are plenty of market stalls in and around the East End. Many sell fruit bought cheaply near the end of trading time from Covent Garden fruit market. The pastry (paste) used in this pie contains ground almonds, which complement the juicy ripe cherries beautifully.

SERVES 6

For the pastry:
200 g/7 oz/1¾ cups plain (all-purpose) flour
A pinch of salt
5 ml/1 tsp caster (superfine) sugar
100 g/4 oz/½ cup butter, cubed
25 g/1 oz/¼ cup ground almonds
1 egg yolk
30–45 ml/2–3 tbsp cold water
For the filling:
50 g/2 oz/¼ cup caster (superfine) sugar
15 ml/1 tbsp cornflour (cornstarch)
900 g/2 lb cherries, stoned (pitted)
15 ml/1 tbsp cherry brandy or orange liqueur (optional)
1 beaten egg, to glaze
Custard or whipped cream, to serve

1 Sift the flour, salt and sugar into a mixing bowl. Add the butter and rub in until the mixture resembles breadcrumbs. Stir in the ground almonds. Mix together the egg yolk and water, sprinkle over, then mix together to make a firm dough.

2 Lightly knead the pastry on a floured surface for a few seconds until smooth. Wrap in clingfilm (plastic wrap) and chill in the fridge for 30 minutes.

3 Mix together the sugar and cornflour, then add the cherries and toss to coat. Sprinkle over the brandy or liqueur, if using, and mix again. Turn the cherries into a pie dish. The cherries should be piled into a slight mound; if there isn't quite enough filling to do this in your dish, put a pie funnel in the centre.

4 Roll out the pastry to a round about 5 cm/2 in larger than the pie dish. Cut off a 2.5 cm/1 in strip from around the edge. Moisten the rim of the pie dish and position the strip on the rim, then lightly brush with water.

5 Lift the pastry lid into position and press the edges together to seal. Trim off any excess pastry and make a couple of steam-holes in the top of the pie. Flute the edges and use the pastry trimmings to make leaves or other pastry decorations.

6 Brush with beaten egg to glaze and bake in a preheated oven at 200°C/400°F/gas mark 6 for 20 minutes. Reduce the oven temperature to 180°C/350°F/gas mark 4 and bake for a further 20 minutes or until the pastry is golden.

7 Serve with custard or whipped cream.

🕐 **Preparation and cooking time:** 1 hour plus chilling

Creamy Rice Pudding

SERVES 4
50 g/2 oz/¼ cup pudding rice
25 g/1 oz/2 tbsp caster (superfine) sugar
A pinch of freshly grated nutmeg
600 ml/1 pt/2½ cups milk

1 Briefly rinse the rice in a sieve (strainer) under cold running water and drain well. Put in a well-buttered 900 ml/ 1½ pt/3¾ cup ovenproof dish.

2 Sprinkle the sugar and nutmeg over, then stir in the milk. Leave to soak for 20 minutes.

3 Put in a cold oven, then turn the oven to 150°C/300°F/ gas mark 2. Bake for 2 hours, stirring after 45 minutes, until the rice is tender and the mixture thick.

🕐 **Preparation and cooking time:** 2¼ hours plus soaking

Economical Fruit Cake

Sunday teas in the East End were a special treat laid on the table with a proper tablecloth and would usually consist of sandwiches, seafood, such as winkles and shrimps, and a fruit cake. When times were hard, an eggless cake like the one in this recipe might be made, in which a combination of vinegar and bicarbonate of soda (baking soda) acted as the raising agent. Don't be deceived by the economical ingredients, however: the taste and texture are every bit as good as the real thing.

Makes 8 large slices
350 g/12 oz/3 cups plain (all-purpose) flour
A pinch of salt
5 ml/1 tsp mixed (apple-pie) spice
175 g/6 oz/¾ cup butter or margarine, diced
175 g/6 oz/scant 1 cup soft light brown sugar
350 g/12 oz/1½ cups dried mixed fruit (fruit cake mix)
10 ml/2 tsp bicarbonate of soda
10 ml/2 tsp vinegar
150 ml/¼ pt/⅔ cup milk
150 ml/¼ pt/⅔ cup water
15 ml/1 tbsp demerara or granulated sugar

1 Grease and line the base and sides of a 20 cm/8 in round cake tin (pan) with greaseproof (waxed) paper or non-stick baking parchment. Preheat the oven to 160°C/325°F/ gas mark 3.

2 Sift the flour, salt and mixed spice into a bowl. Rub in the butter or margarine until the mixture resembles breadcrumbs. Stir in the sugar and dried fruit and make a well in the middle of the mixture.

3 Blend the bicarbonate of soda with the vinegar, milk and water. Add to the dry ingredients, mix thoroughly, then transfer to the tin and make a slightly hollow in the centre. Sprinkle the top with the demerara or granulated sugar.

4 Bake straight away on the middle shelf of the oven for 1½ hours or until well risen, lightly browned and a fine skewer inserted into the centre of the cake comes out clean.

5 Leave the cake in the tin for 15 minutes, then turn out and leave to cool completely on a wire rack. Cut into thick slices to serve.

🕐 **Preparation and cooking time:** 2 hours

➤ **Cook's tip**
To store, wrap the cake in greaseproof paper, then foil. It will keep for up to 2 weeks.

> *The fire was blazing brightly under the influence of the bellows, and the kettle was singing gaily under the influence of both. A small tray of tea things was arranged on the table ...*
> Charles Dickens, *Pickwick Papers*

Iced London Buns

These plain, long, finger buns with white icing (frosting) have been sold by London bakers and street vendors since the eighteenth century. In this more modern version, the dough is enriched with butter and eggs.

MAKES 16
550 g/1¼ lb/4½ cups strong plain (bread) flour
7.5 ml/1½ tsp salt
10 ml/2 tsp easy-blend dried yeast
30 ml/2 tbsp caster (superfine) sugar
40 g/1½ oz butter
150 ml/¼ pt/⅔ cup milk
150 ml/¼ pt/⅔ cup water
2 eggs, lightly beaten
A little milk, to glaze
For the icing:
225 g/8 oz/1⅓ cups icing (confectioners') sugar
2.5 ml/½ tsp vanilla essence (extract)
30–45 ml/2–3 tbsp hot water

1 Sift the flour and salt into a mixing bowl. Stir in the yeast. Make a well in the middle.

2 Gently heat the sugar, butter and milk in a saucepan, stirring occasionally until the sugar has dissolved and the butter melted. Remove from the heat.

3 Stir in the water, then add the eggs and whisk together to combine. Pour into the dry ingredients and mix to a soft, slightly sticky dough.

4 Knead on a lightly floured surface for 10 minutes until smooth and elastic. Put in a bowl, cover with a tea towel (dish cloth) and leave in a warm place to rise for 1½ hours, or until doubled in size.

5 Knock back (punch down) the dough and divide into 16 pieces. Shape each into a finger 10 cm/4 in long. Arrange in two rows on a greased baking (cookie) sheet, spaced slightly apart.

6 Cover with oiled clingfilm (plastic wrap) and leave in a warm place for about 30 minutes until doubled in size. Brush the tops with milk.

7 Bake in a preheated oven at 220°C/425°F/gas mark 7 for 15–20 minutes until golden and hollow-sounding when tapped underneath. Leave to cool on a wire rack, then carefully pull the buns apart if they have joined together during cooking.

8 Sift the icing sugar into a bowl. Add the vanilla essence. Using a wooden spoon, gradually stir in the hot water until the icing has the consistency of thick cream. Spoon over the buns and leave to set before serving.

⏲ **Preparation and cooking time:** 50 minutes plus rising

Seed Cake

*Until Edwardian times this was one of the most popular cakes
served in England. Caraway seeds give it a warm spicy flavour and
crunchy texture.*

MAKES ONE 18 CM/7 IN CAKE

150 g/5 oz/good ½ cup butter, softened
150 g/5 oz/good ½ cup caster (superfine) sugar
2.5 ml/½ tsp ground cinnamon
2 eggs, separated
225 g/8 oz/2 cups plain (all-purpose) flour
A pinch of salt
5 ml/1 tsp baking powder
30 ml/2 tbsp milk
15 ml/1 tbsp caraway seeds

1 Grease and line the base of an 18 cm/7 in round cake
tin (pan).

2 Cream the butter, sugar and cinnamon together until
light and fluffy. Beat in the egg yolks, one at a time.

3 Sift the flour, salt and baking powder over the mixture.
Add the milk and caraway seeds and fold in with a metal spoon.

4 Whisk the egg whites until stiff, but not dry. Carefully
fold in the mixture, half at a time. Spoon into the prepared
cake tin and level the top.

5 Bake on the centre shelf of a preheated oven at
180°C/350°F/gas mark 4 for 1¼ hours or until a skewer
inserted into the centre of the cake comes out clean.

6 Allow the cake to cool in the tin for 15 minutes, then
turn out on to a wire rack.

🕐 **Preparation and cooking time:** 1½ hours

➤ **Cook's tip**
Check the cake after 45 minutes of cooking time; if the top is
starting to brown too much, cover with a piece of foil.

> *It was the pleasantest tea-table in the world. Miss Clarissa presided. I cut and handed the sweet seed cake – the little sisters had a bird-like fondness for picking up seeds and pecking at sugar.*
>
> Charles Dickens, *David Copperfield*

Bread Pudding

MAKES 16 SLICES
450 g/1 lb slightly stale bread, crusts removed
Finely grated rind of 1 orange (optional)
300 ml/½ pt/1¼ cups milk
225 g/8 oz/1⅓ cups mixed dried fruit (fruit cake mix)
75 g/3 oz/⅓ cup butter or margarine, softened
100 g/4 oz/½ cup soft brown sugar
10 ml/2 tsp mixed (apple-pie) spice
15 ml/1 tbsp demerara or granulated sugar

1 Break the bread into small pieces and put in a bowl. Add the orange rind, if using, the milk and fruit. Stir together, then leave to soak for 15 minutes.

2 Meanwhile, stir the butter or margarine, soft brown sugar and spice together until blended, but do not beat. Add the soaked bread and mix well.

3 Spoon the mixture into a greased and lined 18 × 28 cm/ 7 × 11 in cake tin (pan). Level the surface and sprinkle with the demerara or granulated sugar.

4 Bake in a preheated oven at 190°C/375°F/gas mark 5 for 1¼ hours or until firm. Leave to cool in the tin, then turn out and cut into 16 slices.

⏱ **Preparation and cooking time:** 1½ hours

Muffins

These English muffins, or yeasted teacakes, are completely different from the more cake-like American-style muffins. To toast them, cut in half horizontally, then close together again and toast under a low grill (broiler) until warmed through, before opening out and buttering. Don't toast the halves separately, or they may become dry and tough. As late as the 1920s, muffin men used to walk the streets with trays of hot muffins, ringing a bell and calling out to customers.

MAKES 10
450 g/1 lb/4 cups strong plain (bread) flour
5 ml/1 tsp salt
7.5 ml/1½ tsp easy-blend dried yeast
300 ml/½ pt/1¼ cups warm milk
5 ml/1 tsp plain (all-purpose) flour, for dusting
5 ml/1 tsp fine semolina (cream of wheat)

1 Sift the flour and salt into a mixing bowl. Stir in the yeast and make a well in the middle. Pour in the milk and mix to a soft dough.

2 Knead on a lightly floured surface for 10 minutes until smooth and elastic. Put in a clean bowl, cover with a tea towel (dish cloth) or clingfilm (plastic wrap) and leave in a warm place for abut 1 hour until doubled in size.

3 Roll out the dough to 1 cm/½ in thick. Cover with a tea towel and leave to rest for 10 minutes. Cut into rounds using a 7.5 cm/3 in plain cutter and place well apart on a floured baking (cookie) sheet.

4 Mix together the flour and semolina and dust over the tops of the muffins. Cover with a tea towel and leave in a warm place for 20–25 minutes or until doubled in size.

5 Grease a heavy frying pan (skillet) or griddle and heat over a moderate heat. When hot, cook the muffins for 6–8 minutes on each side until golden brown and cooked through. Serve warm.

⊕ **Preparation and cooking time:** 40 minutes plus rising

Sticky Treacle Tart

When making shortcrust pastry (basic pie crust), it was traditional to use half butter for colour and flavour and half lard (shortening) to give the pastry (paste) its short, crumbly texture. All butter may be used if preferred for a richer flavour.

SERVES 8

For the pastry:
225 g/8 oz/2 cups plain (all-purpose) flour
A pinch of salt
100 g/4 oz/½ cup butter or 50 g/2 oz/¼ cup each lard or white
    vegetable fat and butter or margarine
45–60 ml/3–4 tbsp iced water
For the filling:
700 g/1½ lb/2 cups golden (light corn) syrup
175 g/6 oz/3 cups fresh white breadcrumbs
Finely grated rind of 1 lemon
2 eggs, lightly beaten
Whipped cream or ice cream, to serve

1 Sift the flour and salt into a mixing bowl and rub in the fat until the mixture resembles fine breadcrumbs. Sprinkle the water over the dry ingredients and mix to a firm dough.

2 Lightly knead the pastry on a floured surface for a few seconds. Wrap and chill for 20 minutes.

3 Roll out the pastry and use to line a 25 cm/10 in fluted, loose-bottomed flan tin (pie pan) about 4 cm/1½ in deep. Prick the base with a fork and chill while preparing the filling.

4 Gently heat the golden syrup in a saucepan until runny. Remove from the heat and stir in the breadcrumbs and lemon rind. Stir in the eggs until thoroughly mixed. Pour into the pastry case (pie shell).

5 Bake in a preheated oven at 180°C/350°F/gas mark 4 for 45 minutes or until the filling is lightly set. Serve warm with whipped cream or ice cream.

🕐 **Preparation and cooking time:** 1¼ hours plus chilling

Jam Tarts

*When cheap and plentiful, fruit was preserved and served with
bread and dripping or used to fill tarts. These would usually be
made with plain shortcrust (basic pie crust), but a richer pastry
(paste) can be used, as in this tasty version.*

MAKES 12

100 g/4 oz/1 cup plain (all-purpose) flour
50 g/2 oz/¼ cup butter or margarine, chilled and diced
25 g/1 oz/2 tbsp icing (confectioners') sugar, sifted
1 egg yolk
15 ml/1 tbsp cold water
175 ml/6 oz/¾ cup jam (conserve), any flavour

1 Sift the flour into a bowl. Using your fingertips, rub the
butter or margarine into the flour until the mixture
resembles fine breadcrumbs. Stir in the icing sugar.

2 Mix the egg yolk and water together, sprinkle over the
flour mixture and mix to a dough. Lightly knead on a floured
surface for a few seconds until smooth. Wrap in clingfilm
(plastic wrap) and chill in the fridge for 20 minutes.

3 Roll out the pastry and cut out 12 rounds, using a
fluted 7.5 cm/3 in cutter. Place in lightly greased patty tins
(pans) and put a tablespoonful of jam in each.

4 Bake in a preheated oven at 200°C/400°F/gas mark 6
for 15 minutes or until the pastry is golden brown. Leave in
the tins for 5 minutes before transferring to a wire rack to
cool. Serve warm or cold.

⏱ **Preparation and cooking time:** 40 minutes plus chilling

Gingerbread Men

The gingerbread seller with his tray of spicy biscuits was a popular figure on London's streets.

MAKES 6

175 g/6 oz/1½ cups plain (all-purpose) flour
2.5 ml/½ tsp bicarbonate of soda (baking soda)
5 ml/1 tsp ground ginger
50 g/2 oz/¼ cup butter, diced
75 g/3 oz/⅓ cup soft brown sugar
30 ml/2 tbsp golden (light corn) syrup
½ egg, lightly beaten
Currants and glacé (candied) cherries, to decorate

1 Sift the flour, bicarbonate of soda and ginger into a mixing bowl. Rub in the butter until the mixture resembles fine breadcrumbs. Stir in the sugar.

2 Stir together the golden syrup and egg. Add to the dry ingredients and mix to a dough. Lightly knead on a floured surface until smooth.

3 Roll out the dough until 5 mm/¼ in thick. Cut out gingerbread men, using a cutter if you have one, and transfer to a lightly greased baking (cookie) sheet. Gently press in currants and chopped glacé cherries to represent eyes, buttons and mouths.

4 Bake in a preheated oven at 190ºC/375ºF/gas mark 5 for 12–15 minutes until golden. Leave on the baking sheet for 2–3 minutes, then transfer to a wire rack to cool.

⏱ **Preparation and cooking time:** 30 minutes

Junket

The setting agent, rennet, is sold as a liquid or a tablet. Only use ordinary pasteurised milk for this dessert and take care not to overheat the milk or to disturb the junket while it cools or it will not set properly.

SERVES 4

600 ml/1 pt/2½ cups pasteurised full-cream milk
15 ml/1 tbsp caster (superfine) sugar
5 ml/1 tsp liquid rennet
1.5 ml/¼ tsp freshly grated nutmeg

1 Put the milk and sugar in a saucepan and heat until it is just warm. Stir to dissolve the sugar, then add the rennet and stir again.

2 Pour into a shallow serving bowl and leave for 1–2 hours at room temperature, undisturbed, until set.

3 Sprinkle the top with grated nutmeg and chill in the fridge until ready to serve.

🕐 **Preparation and cooking time:** 10 minutes plus setting

➤ **Cook's tip**
You can flavour the junket, if liked, by stirring 30 ml/2 tbsp rum or 5 ml/1 tsp vanilla essence (extract) into the warm milk, before adding the rennet.

Spotted Dick

This steamed suet sponge, subtly flavoured with lemon rind and packed with currants, was a great favourite, good for filling up a hungry family, especially when accompanied by a generous serving of custard.

SERVES 4

100 g/4 oz/1 cup self-raising (self-rising) flour
A pinch of salt
100 g/4 oz/2 cups fresh white breadcrumbs
100 g/4 oz/1 cup shredded (chopped) suet
50 g/2 oz/¼ cup caster (superfine) sugar
75 g/3 oz/½ cup currants
Finely grated rind of 1 lemon
About 150 ml/¼ pt/⅔ cup milk
Custard, to serve

1 Sift the flour and salt into a mixing bowl. Stir in the breadcrumbs, suet, sugar, currants and lemon rind. Add most of the milk and mix to a soft dropping consistency, adding a little more milk if needed.

2 Spoon the mixture into a base-lined, well-buttered 900 ml/1½ pt/3¾ cup pudding basin. Place a double thickness of greaseproof (waxed) paper, pleated in the centre, over the pudding, then place a similarly pleated piece of foil over the top and tie with string (the pleats give room for the pudding to rise).

3 Put the basin on a trivet in a saucepan and pour in enough boiling water to come halfway up the side of the basin. Cover the pan and steam for 2 hours, topping up with boiling water as necessary.

4 Remove the basin from the pan and ease round the edge of the pudding with a round-bladed knife. Turn the pudding out on to a warmed plate. Cut into wedges and serve with steaming hot custard.

⏱ **Preparation and cooking time:** 2¼ hours

Roly-poly Pudding

This rolled-up pudding can be filled in a number of ways; jam (conserve) as used here is one of the most popular, but golden (light corn) syrup, mixed with fresh white breadcrumbs, or a lemon curd filling works equally well. One version, known as 'Black Jack', is made with currants and may have been named after Jack the Ripper, who murdered and dismembered seven prostitutes in four months between August and November 1888. A morbid interest in this crime has remained, perhaps because the identity of the Ripper was never discovered. A sightseeing trip in the East End invariably includes visits to the scenes where these gruesome murders were committed.

SERVES 4–6

175 g/6 oz/1½ cups self-raising (self-rising) flour
A pinch of salt
75 g/3 oz/¾ cup shredded (chopped) suet
About 100 ml/3½ fl oz/scant ½ cup cold water
75 ml/5 tbsp jam, any flavour
15 ml/1 tbsp milk

1 Sift the flour and salt into a bowl and stir in the suet. Add the water and mix to a soft dough, using a round-bladed knife, adding a little extra liquid if the mixture is slightly dry.

2 Knead for a few seconds on a lightly floured surface until smooth, then roll out to a rectangle about 23 × 28 cm/ 9 × 11 in.

3 Spread the dough with the jam, leaving a 2 cm/¾ in border around the edges. Brush the edges with milk and roll up, starting from a short end.

4 Transfer the roly-poly to a lightly greased baking (cookie) sheet and bake in a preheated oven at 200°C/400°F/ gas mark 6 for 35–40 minutes. Serve thickly sliced with custard.

⏱ **Preparation and cooking time:** 50 minutes

Hot Baked Wardens

Hot and spicy baked pears, known as 'wardens', were once sold from huge earthernware dishes by street vendors.

SERVES 6

6 just-ripe pears
30 ml/2 tbsp lemon juice
175 g/6 oz/¾ cup granulated sugar
A pinch of saffron threads
4 whole cloves
1 cinnamon stick
2.5 cm/1 in piece of fresh root ginger, peeled and sliced
450 ml/¾ pt/2 cups water

1 Peel the pears, leaving them whole, with the stalks still on. With the tip of a potato peeler or a sharp knife, scoop out the core end from the base of each. Brush with the lemon juice to prevent them turning brown.

2 Put all the remaining ingredients in a saucepan and bring to the boil, stirring until the sugar has dissolved. Pour into an ovenproof dish and add the pears, packed in tightly.

3 Cover with a piece of greaseproof (waxed) paper to keep the pears submerged, then with a lid. Bake at 180°C/350°F/ gas mark 4 for 20–25 minutes until the pears are tender.

4 Remove the pears and place in a serving dish. Boil the syrup for 5 minutes to reduce slightly and to concentrate the flavours, then strain over the pears. Serve hot.

⏲ **Preparation and cooking time:** 45 minutes

Smoking hot, piping hot
Who knows what I've got in my pot?
Hot baked wardens
All hot, all hot, all hot!

London street cry

Hot Cross Buns

In the early nineteenth century, a widow saved a hot cross bun for her sailor son, expected home at Easter. He never returned, but the widow didn't give up hope and saved a hot cross bun for him every year until she died. This custom is continued at the Widow's Son pub in Devons Road, Bromley-by-Bow, in the East End of London, right in the centre of the docklands. It is not known whether the widow was the pub landlady or if the house where she lived was knocked down and the pub built in its place, but the practice is now a condition of the lease. Every Good Friday, a serving sailor hangs up a bun and there are now over 200 buns there (the more decayed ones are stored in the cellar). Free hot cross buns are still given to everyone in the pub and to children who gather hopefully outside.

MAKES 12

A strip of thinly pared lemon or orange rind
175 ml/6 fl oz/¾ cup milk
350 g/12 oz/3 cups strong (plain) bread flour
5 ml/1 tsp salt
5 ml/1 tsp mixed (apple-pie) spice
5 ml/1 tsp ground cinnamon
50 g/2 oz/¼ cup butter or margarine, cubed
7.5 ml/1½ tsp easy-blend dried yeast
50 g/2 oz/¼ cup caster (superfine) sugar
100 g/4 oz/⅔ cup dried mixed fruit (fruit cake mix)
1 egg, lightly beaten
A little milk, to glaze

1 Put the lemon or orange rind in a small saucepan with the milk and heat gently until hot. Turn off the heat, cover with a lid and leave until lukewarm.

2 Sift the flour, salt and spices into a mixing bowl. Rub in the butter or margarine until the mixture resembles fine breadcrumbs. Stir in the yeast, 25 g/1 oz/2 tbsp of the sugar and the fruit. Make a well in the middle.

3 Remove the rind from the milk and discard. Pour the flavoured milk into the dry ingredients, add the egg and mix to a dough.

4 Knead on a lightly floured surface for 10 minutes until smooth and elastic. Place in an oiled bowl, cover with clingfilm (plastic wrap) and leave in a warm place for about 1½ hours or until doubled in size.

5 Knock back (punch down) the dough and divide into 12 equal pieces. Shape each into a ball and place well apart on a large greased baking (cookie) sheet, flattening each slightly.

6 Make a deep cross on each one with a sharp knife. Cover with oiled clingfilm and leave to rise for about 20 minutes until doubled in size.

7 Brush the tops with milk, then bake in a preheated oven at 200°C/400°F/gas mark 6 for 10 minutes. Turn down the oven to 190°C/375°F/gas mark 5 and bake for a further 5–10 minutes until the buns are golden brown and sound hollow when tapped underneath.

8 Meanwhile, put the remaining sugar in a small pan with 30 ml/2 tbsp water and heat gently until the sugar dissolves. Brush over the hot buns. Cool on a wire rack and eat within 2 days.

🕐 **Preparation and cooking time:** 50 minutes plus rising

Hot cross buns, hot cross buns,
One a penny, two a penny,
Hot cross buns.
If you have no daughters, give them to your sons.
One a penny, two a penny,
Hot cross buns.

Traditional nursery rhyme

Baked Apple Dumplings

SERVES 4

For the pastry (paste):
225 g/8 oz/2 cups plain (all-purpose) flour
A pinch of salt
100 g/4 oz/½ cup butter or margarine
2 egg yolks
60 ml/4 tbsp cold water
For the apple filling:
4 firm cooking (tart) apples, peeled
1 egg white
25 g/1 oz/2 tbsp butter or margarine, softened
50 g/2 oz/¼ cup soft light brown sugar
2.5 ml/½ tsp ground cinnamon
15 ml/1 tbsp caster (superfine) sugar

1 Sift the flour and salt into a mixing bowl, then rub in the butter or margarine until the mixture resembles fine breadcrumbs. Mix the egg yolks and water together, sprinkle over the dry ingredients and mix to a firm dough.

2 Lightly knead the pastry on a floured surface for a few seconds until smooth, then wrap in clingfilm (plastic wrap) and chill in the fridge for 30 minutes.

3 Remove the cores from the apples. Roll out three-quarters of the pastry and cut into four squares, almost large enough to enclose the apples.

4 Brush the pastry with egg white and place an apple in the middle of each. Blend the butter or margarine, brown sugar and cinnamon together and spoon into the hollows of the apples.

5 Roll out the remaining pastry and cut into four 5 cm/2 in rounds. Place a pastry round on top of each apple, brush it with egg white, then bring up the sides of the pastry square to enclose it, pleating to fit.

6 Roll out the pastry trimmings and cut out leaves to decorate the dumplings. Brush with egg white and sprinkle with caster sugar. Place on a baking (cookie) sheet and make a steam-hole in the top of each.

7 Bake the dumplings in a preheated oven at 220°C/425°F/gas mark 7 for 15 minutes, then lower the oven temperature to 180°C/350°F/gas mark 4 and bake for a further 20 minutes or until the pastry is golden brown and the apples tender.

🕐 **Preparation and cooking time:** 50 minutes plus chilling

Toffee Apples

MAKES 8
8 eating (dessert) apples
450 g/1 lb/2 cups demerara sugar
50 g/2 oz/¼ cup butter
5 ml/1 tsp malt vinegar
150 ml/¼ pt/⅔ cup water
15 ml/1 tbsp golden (light corn) syrup

1 Wash and dry the apples, then push a wooden stick into the core of each, making sure that it is secure.

2 Put all the remaining ingredients into a heavy-based saucepan and heat gently until the butter has melted and the sugar has dissolved.

3 Bring to the boil and cook until the syrup registers 138°C/280°F on a sugar thermometer (this is the 'soft crack' stage, when a teaspoon of the mixture dropped into cold water separates into hard but not brittle threads).

4 Remove from the heat. Carefully dip the apples one at a time into the toffee, turning them to coat all over. Let some of the excess drip off, then place on greaseproof (waxed) paper or a well-greased baking (cookie) sheet to cool and set.

🕐 **Preparation and cooking time:** 30 minutes

Treacle Toffee

MAKES ABOUT 750 G/1¾ LB
450 g/1 lb/2 cups demerara sugar
150 ml/¼ pt/⅔ cup water
100 g/4 oz/⅓ cup golden (light corn) syrup
100 g/4 oz/⅓ cup black treacle or molasses
75 g/3 oz/⅓ cup butter
1.5 ml/¼ tsp cream of tartar

1 Grease an 18 cm/7 in square tin (pan) and line the base with baking parchment or greaseproof (waxed) paper. Gently heat the sugar and water in a heavy-based saucepan until dissolved.

2 Add all the remaining ingredients. Bring to the boil and boil steadily until the syrup registers 138°C/280°F on a sugar thermometer (this is the 'soft crack' stage, when a little of the mixture dropped into a small bowl of cold water separates into hard but not brittle threads).

3 Remove from the heat and carefully pour into the prepared tin. Leave to cool for 5 minutes, then mark into squares and leave to set. Break into squares and store in an airtight container.

🕐 **Preparation and cooking time:** 20 minutes

Lemon or lime, penny a bag.
Pepper, penny a pot.
Street sweet trader's cry

Peppermint Humbugs

You can make striped humbugs by colouring half the mixture with a drop of brown food colouring, added with the flavouring. Make two ropes of each colour and twist together before cutting into pieces. It's impossible to work both mixtures together at the same time, however, so you'll need to enlist the help of a friend.

MAKES ABOUT 450 G/1 LB
450 g/1 lb/2 cups granulated sugar
150 ml/¼ pt/⅔ cups water
1.5 ml/¼ tsp cream of tartar
15 ml/1 tbsp golden (light corn) syrup
A few drops of peppermint essence (extract)

1 Lightly oil a marble slab or a wooden chopping board. Put the sugar and water in a large, heavy-based saucepan and heat gently until dissolved.

2 Blend the cream of tartar with 15 ml/1 tbsp water and the golden syrup and add to the saucepan. Simmer until the mixture reaches 155°C/298°F on a sugar thermometer (this is the 'hard crack' stage when a small quantity of mixture dropped in cold water separates into threads that become hard and brittle).

3 Pour the syrup on to the slab and allow to cool a little. Using oiled palette knives, fold the sides of the mixture into the centre and add a few drops of peppermint essence.

4 Keep the mixture moving with the palette knives until it is cool enough to handle. Oil your hands and twist into a rope, fold it back on itself and pull and twist again, continuing until opaque and shiny.

5 Finally, pull out into an even twist about 2.5 cm/1 in thick. Cut off 2.5 cm/1 in pieces with oiled scissors. Leave to cool completely, then store in an airtight container.

🕐 **Preparation and cooking time:** 40 minutes

Celebrations

East Enders still love a 'knees-up', whether it's in the local pub, or at a street party for a royal wedding, coronation or jubilee. At the end of the Second World War, London led the celebrations, as everyone who could rushed to see the King and Queen and the Prime Minister, Winston Churchill, on the balcony of Buckingham Palace, and then joined in the numerous street parties all over the capital.

Of course, food fashion has changed; blancmange is no longer compulsory food at children's parties and fresh lemonade has largely been ousted by fizzy drinks. But Christmas pudding with brandy butter is still an annual treat in most households and for some people nothing will replace a good strong cup of tea!

Knees up, Mother Brown!
Knees up, Mother Brown!
Under the table you must go,
Singing 'Ee-I-addy-oh!'
If I catch you bending,
I'll saw your legs right off,
So knees up, knees up,
Don't get the breeze up,
Knees up, Mother Brown!

Music hall song

Blancmange

The name of this dessert is derived from the French words blanc *and* manger, *meaning 'white' and 'eat'. In medieval times the dish contained minced (ground) chicken, rice and almond milk, but by the seventeenth century it became a sweet dish, similar to the one we know today. In the 1950s and 60s it was a regular feature at children's parties, often made in a rabbit-shaped mould and usually coloured pink!*

SERVES 4

60 ml/4 tbsp cornflour (cornstarch)
600 ml/1 pt/2½ cups milk
A strip of thinly pared lemon rind
25 g/1 oz/2 tbsp caster (superfine) sugar

1 Blend the cornflour with 45 ml/3 tbsp of the milk to make a smooth paste.

2 Put the remaining milk in a saucepan with the lemon rind and sugar. Bring to the boil, then pour over the blended mixture, stirring all the time.

3 Return the mixture to the pan and bring to the boil, stirring all the time, until the mixture is smooth and thick. Gently simmer for 2–3 minutes, then remove the lemon rind.

4 Pour into a dampened 600 ml/1 pt/2½ cup mould and leave to cool. Chill in the fridge for 1–2 hours until set.

5 To serve, dip the mould briefly in hot water to loosen, then turn out on to a serving plate. Return to the fridge until ready to serve.

⊙ **Preparation and cooking time:** 20 minutes plus setting

➤ **Cook's tips**
You can make variations by using different flavours and colouring. For a strawberry blancmange, omit the lemon rind and stir a drop of pink food colouring and 2.5 ml/½ tsp strawberry essence (extract) to the mixture just before pouring into the mould. Serve with fresh strawberries.

Traditional Trifle

There are many versions of trifle, but this unsophisticated one is typical of those that were served at East End street parties. When raspberries weren't in season, they were replaced by canned fruit. An orange liqueur or fruit juice can be used instead of some or all of the sherry.

SERVES 6

8 trifle sponges
60 ml/4 tbsp raspberry jam (conserve)
75 ml/5 tbsp sweet sherry
350 g/12 oz fresh or thawed frozen raspberries
For the custard:
5 ml/1 tsp cornflour (cornstarch)
3 egg yolks
1 whole egg
30 ml/2 tbsp caster (superfine) sugar
2.5 ml/½ tsp vanilla essence (extract)
450 ml/¾ pt/2 cups milk
For the topping:
300 ml/½ pt/1¼ cups whipping cream
15 ml/1 tbsp icing (confectioners') sugar, sifted
25 g/1 oz/¼ cup flaked (slivered) almonds
Silver balls, to decorate (optional)

1 Split the trifle sponge cakes in half, spread one half of each with jam and sandwich them back together. Cut into cubes and place them in a glass or china serving dish. Sprinkle the sherry over the sponges.

2 If using fresh raspberries, reserve a few for decorating. Arrange the rest in an even layer over the sponges, together with any juices if the raspberries were frozen.

3 For the custard, put the cornflour, egg yolks, whole egg, sugar and vanilla essence in a bowl with 30 ml/2 tbsp of the milk and mix together.

4 Heat the remaining milk to boiling point, then pour over the egg mixture, whisking all the time. Return to the saucepan and cook over a gentle heat until thickened, but do not let the mixture boil.

5 Remove from the heat and allow to cool for 10 minutes, stirring occasionally to prevent a skin forming. Pour over the trifle, cover and leave to cool. Chill in the fridge until ready to serve.

6 Whip the cream and icing sugar until soft peaks form. Spoon over the custard, spreading out to cover the top. Scatter with the flaked almonds and silver balls, if using. Decorate with the reserved fresh raspberries.

⊕ **Preparation and cooking time:** 30 minutes plus cooling

Roast Chestnuts

Still sold on street corners, roasted chestnuts have an irresistible aroma on a cold winter's day. Chestnuts have grown wild in Britain for centuries, although they are not indigenous and thrive best in warmer climates; those imported from Italy, France and Spain are much larger and it's usually these nuts that are roasted by street vendors.

Chestnuts can be roasted over an open fire, but for this you will need a chestnut roaster, which looks rather like a frying pan (skillet) with a perforated lid and a long handle.

Slit the tops of the chestnuts with a sharp knife, then put one over each hole in the chestnut roaster. Roast in the fire for 7–8 minutes; they will 'sing' when done. To oven-roast, slit the chestnuts and place in a single layer in a roasting tin (pan). Bake at 200°C/400°F/gas mark 6 for about 15 minutes until slightly charred. Cool for a few minutes before serving.

⊕ **Preparation and cooking time:** 20 minutes

Christmas Pudding

*Even if Christmas dinner was meagre, there would always be a
pudding, made several months before, perhaps at a time when dried
fruits were less expensive. The tradition of serving a Christmas
pudding was introduced to the Victorians by Prince Albert and
burying a silver coin (a sixpence before the days of decimal
currency) is said to bring good fortune to whoever finds it in their
portion. On Stir Up Sunday, the Sunday before Advent, all the family
gave the pudding mixture a stir and made a secret wish. The
pudding would have traditionally been tied in a cloth and boiled.
Before serving, the pudding is set alight with brandy or rum and
brought to the table in a shimmering blue haze.*

SERVES 8

100 g/4 oz/1 cup self-raising (self-rising) flour
5 ml/1 tsp mixed (apple-pie) spice
1.5 ml/¼ tsp salt
225 g/8 oz/1⅓ cups seedless raisins
225 g/8 oz/1⅓ cups sultanas (golden raisins)
75 g/3 oz/½ cup chopped mixed (candied) peel
Finely grated rind of 1 lemon
75 g/3 oz/¾ cup fresh white breadcrumbs
75 g/3 oz/¾ cup shredded (chopped) suet
100 g/4 oz/½ cup dark soft brown sugar
1 carrot, peeled and grated
½ cooking (tart) apple, peeled, cored and grated
2 eggs, lightly beaten
15 ml/1 tbsp black treacle (molasses)
150 ml/¼ pt/⅔ cup milk or brown ale
30 ml/2 tbsp dark rum or brandy
Extra rum or brandy, brandy butter and/or white sauce
   (see page 94), to serve

1 Sift the flour, spice and salt into a large mixing bowl.
Add the dried fruit, peel, lemon rind, breadcrumbs, suet,
sugar, carrot and apple and mix together.

2 Blend the eggs, treacle, milk or ale and rum or brandy,
add to the dry ingredients and stir well.

3 Grease and line the base of a 1.5 litre/2½ pt/6 cup pudding basin. Spoon in the mixture and press down well. Cover the basin with greaseproof (waxed) paper and foil, pleated in the centre to allow the pudding room to rise a little. Secure under the rim with string.

4 Put the pudding on a trivet or upturned saucer in a saucepan and pour in enough boiling water to come halfway up the sides of the basin. Cover the pan tightly and simmer gently for 4 hours, topping up the pan with boiling water as necessary.

5 Lift the pudding basin out of the pan and leave to cool, then re-cover with fresh greaseproof paper and foil. Store in a cool, dark place for at least 6 weeks.

6 On the day, steam (see step 4) for about 2 hours. Turn out on to a warmed serving plate. Warm about 60 ml/4 tbsp rum or brandy in a saucepan, pour over the pudding and set alight. When the flames have gone out, cut into wedges and serve with brandy butter or white sauce.

⏱ **Preparation and cooking time:** 4½ hours plus storing

Mrs Cratchit entered – flushed, but smiling proudly – with the pudding, like a speckled cannon-ball, so hard and firm, blazing in half of half-a-quartern of ignited brandy, and bedight with Christmas holly stuck into the top.
'Oh, a wonderful pudding!' Bob Cratchit said, and calmly too, that he regarded it as the greatest success achieved by Mrs Cratchit since their marriage ...
Everyone had something to say about it, but nobody said or thought it was at all a small pudding for a large family.

Charles Dickens, *A Christmas Carol*

Brandy Butter

SERVES 8
100 g/4 oz/½ cup unsalted (sweet) butter, softened
100 g/4 oz/½ cup soft light brown sugar
90 ml/6 tbsp brandy

1 Beat the butter until soft, then gradually beat in the sugar until light and fluffy.

2 Beat in the brandy, 15 ml/1 tbsp at a time. Transfer to a serving bowl and chill in the fridge until needed.

⏲ **Preparation time:** 15 minutes

White Sauce

This is a plain sauce that makes an ideal contrast with very rich Christmas pudding. This quantity will serve about 4–6 people.

MAKES 750 ML/1¼ PTS/3 CUPS
60 ml/4 tbsp cornflour (cornstarch)
45 ml/3 tbsp caster (superfine) sugar
750 ml/1¼ pts/3 cups milk
5 ml/1 tsp vanilla essence (extract)

1 Blend the cornflour, sugar and 30 ml/2 tbsp milk.

2 Heat the rest of the milk to boiling point, then pour over the cornflour mixture, whisking all the time.

3 Return to the saucepan and simmer for 2 minutes, stirring all the time until thickened and smooth. Stir in the vanilla essence and serve straight away.

⏲ **Preparation and cooking time:** 10 minutes

Tea

Tea is still the most popular beverage in Britain, despite fierce competition in recent years from both ground and instant coffee. When it was first introduced in the 1650s it was a luxury, but as the tea trade grew, it became more affordable and was soon the nation's favourite drink, enjoyed by rich and poor alike. Cockneys liked their tea strong and sweet, often adding condensed milk, which could be kept without refrigeration. In the 1930s, tea could be bought in penny packets from the corner grocer, much of it coming from the 'sweepings' of the huge tea warehouses in the docks, which were destroyed in the Blitz of the Second World War.

To make a pot of tea, fill a kettle with fresh, cold water and bring to the boil. As the kettle heats, swill a little hot water around the teapot to warm it, then pour it away. Add the tea leaves to the pot; according to the old saying, you should allow one teaspoonful per person 'and one for the pot', although this clearly depends on the type of tea and your personal preference. When the kettle starts to boil, pour the water on to the tea leaves. Put on the teapot lid, cover with a cosy and leave the tea to brew for 4–5 minutes. Pour through a tea strainer into mugs or cups. There is some controversy as to whether the milk should be added before or after the tea is poured. Adding it before protects more delicate cups from cracking under the heat of the near-boiling tea, but purists would argue that only by adding it afterwards can you assess the exact amount you need.

🕐 **Preparation time:** 10 minutes

Plum Cake

A rich fruit cake, made well in advance and liberally dosed with alcohol is always centrepiece at tea on Christmas Day and other important occasions such as weddings and christenings. The name 'plum' originally referred to the prunes that were chopped and added to the mixture, but it soon came to refer to any dried fruit.

MAKES ONE 20 CM/8 IN ROUND OR 18 CM/7 IN SQUARE CAKE

175 g/6 oz/1 cup currants
175 g/6 oz/1 cup seedless raisins
175 g/6 oz/1 cup sultanas (golden raisins)
75 g/3 oz/½ cup stoned (pitted) prunes, chopped
50 g/2 oz/¼ cup glacé (candied) cherries, chopped
75 g/3 oz/½ cup mixed (candied) peel, chopped
Finely grated rind and juice of 1 small lemon
Finely grated rind and juice of ½ orange
100 ml/3½ fl oz/scant ½ cup dark rum, brandy or sherry
175 g/6 oz/¾ cup butter or margarine, softened
150 g/5 oz/good ½ cup dark soft brown sugar
3 eggs, lightly beaten
15 ml/1 tbsp black treacle (molasses)
30 ml/2 tbsp fine-cut orange marmalade
200 g/7 oz/1¾ cups plain (all-purpose) flour
2.5 ml/½ tsp baking powder
2.5 ml/½ tsp ground cinnamon
5 ml/1 tsp mixed (apple-pie) spice
50 g/2 oz/½ cup walnuts, chopped

1 The day before, place all the fruit, the mixed peel, the lemon and orange rind and juice and the rum, brandy or sherry in a bowl. Mix together, cover with clingfilm (plastic wrap) and leave to soak overnight.

2 The following day, grease the base and sides of your chosen cake tin (pan) and line with greaseproof (waxed) paper. Put the butter or margarine and sugar in a large bowl and beat together until light and fluffy.

3 Blend the eggs, treacle and marmalade together and gradually add to the creamed mixture, a little at a time, beating well between each addition.

4 Sift over the flour, baking powder, cinnamon and mixed spice and fold in, then stir in the soaked fruit and walnuts. Spoon the mixture into the prepared tin and smooth the top, making a very slight dip in the middle, so that it rises evenly.

5 Wrap and tie a double-thickness strip of brown paper around the outside of the tin to prevent the sides of the cake over-browning. Bake in a preheated oven at 140°C/275°F/gas mark 1 for 3 hours or until a skewer inserted into the centre comes out clean.

6 Remove the cake from the oven and leave in the tin for 20 minutes. Turn out on to a wire rack to cool completely. Do not remove the lining paper. Wrap the cake in greaseproof paper, then in foil, and store for at least 6 weeks before serving.

🕐 **Preparation and cooking time:** 3½ hours plus soaking

➤ **Cook's tip**
For a really moist, delicious cake, 'feed' the cake weekly. Pierce the surface of the cake all over with a very fine skewer before sprinkling with 30–45 ml/2–3 tbsp dark rum or brandy, then rewrap the cake.

Glazed Ham

Traditional East End funerals are 'celebrated' in style and it is customary to have four black horses with plumes of feathers on their heads, pulling the hearse. Afterwards a lavish cold buffet is served, usually including a glazed ham. The joint is boiled, which removes any excess salt and keeps the joint wonderfully moist, before baking. It was often served with pease pudding. You can make your own, but it's a lot easier to use a can!

SERVES ABOUT 20

3.5 kg/8 lb ham or gammon
1 onion, thickly sliced
2 celery sticks, thickly sliced
2 carrots, thickly sliced
2 bay leaves
4 large sprigs of parsley
6 black peppercorns
10 ml/2 tsp made English mustard
45 ml/3 tbsp light soft brown sugar
300 ml/½ pt/1¼ cups cider
About 20 whole cloves
Pickles, to serve

1 Soak the ham or gammon in cold water overnight, then put in a large saucepan with the vegetables, bay leaves, parsley and peppercorns and cover with cold water.

2 Bring to the boil, then reduce the heat, cover and simmer very gently for 2½ hours, skimming off any froth that rises to the surface.

3 Turn off the heat, pour in a couple of cups of cold water to stop the cooking, then leave the ham to cool in the water for 20 minutes.

4 Lift out of the water and place in a roasting tin (pan). Remove the rind and score the fat in a diamond pattern. Mix the mustard, sugar and a little of the cider to a thick paste. Spread evenly over the fat and stud each diamond with a clove. Pour the rest of the cider into the tin.

5 Bake in a preheated oven at 180°C/350°F/gas mark 4 for 35–40 minutes, basting occasionally with the cider. Transfer to a plate and allow to cool completely before carving and serving with pickles.

🕐 **Preparation and cooking time:** 3½ hours plus soaking

The four sat down to breakfast, on the coffee, and some hot rolls and ham which the Dodger had brought home in the crown of his hat.

Charles Dickens, *Oliver Twist*

Sloe Gin

A day trip to the countryside at the end of summer might include picking sloes to make this wonderful warming winter drink, which matures just in time for Christmas. Note that sloes are too bitter to be suitable for pies or jam (conserve).

MAKES 1 LITRE/1¾ PTS/4¼ CUPS

1 litre bottle of gin
175 g/6 oz/1 cup sloes, washed and dried
100 g/4 oz/½ cup caster (superfine) sugar

1 Pour the gin into a larger bottle with a screw top. Prick the sloes all over with a darning needle or fine skewer and add to the gin with the sugar.

2 Screw on the cap tightly and gently shake to start the sugar dissolving.

3 Store the bottle on its side in a cool, dark place. Turn the bottle every day for the first 6 weeks, then leave to stand undisturbed for at least 4 more weeks before sampling. Drink within 1 year of making.

🕐 **Preparation time:** 30 minutes plus maturing

Leftover and Economy Meals

There were, of course, well-off cockneys who ran thriving businesses in the East End, but for many 'making do' was a way of life. Thrifty housewives made the most of cheaper cuts of meat and leftovers, and meals included lots of filling extras such as dumplings. In the days before refrigeration, late Saturday afternoon was a good time to buy the Sunday joint as butchers sold off the stock they would be unable to store over the weekend while the shop was closed. The joint would not only feed the family on Sunday, but would be stretched out to cold cuts on Monday and probably minced (ground) for Tuesday as well. Nothing was wasted; even the dripping from the roast meat was served (and much enjoyed), spread on bread or toast.

Many imitation recipes were invented, especially during the war years when 'mock crab' and 'mock duck' were popular. Fresh meat was augmented or replaced with corned beef and plenty of home-grown vegetables. When sugar was rationed, cakes would contain other ingredients that added sweetness, such as grated or puréed root vegetables, including parsnips and carrots (carrot cake is still a favourite today).

During the London Blitz, there were weeks when the city was bombed both day and night. Many people sheltered in underground shelters at tube stations and inexpensive snacks such as simple pasties and hot drinks were provided by J Lyons of Cadby Hall.

Bubble and Squeak

This recipe used up leftover cooked potatoes and cabbage, and included meat when available. The name comes from the lovely sounds it makes while cooking! It was often served to children at teatime, and has always been a traditional Boxing Day favourite. Although many charitable organisations were set up in the East End to help the poor, the Fern Street Settlement in Bromley-by-Bow, established in 1907 by Clara Grant, was specifically for children. She provided small parcels of inexpensive toys for those who had virtually nothing. So that this wouldn't be considered 'charity', the children paid for their gift with the smallest coin, which at that time was a farthing. They gathered in their hundreds every Saturday morning to 'buy' their parcels, girls one week and boys the next. In order to qualify, they had to be small enough to walk under a four-foot wooden arch, inscribed with the words: 'Enter all ye children small, none can come who are too tall'. The height of the arch has been raised several times as has the price – it is now 1p.

SERVES 2

25 g/1 oz/2 tbsp butter or margarine
5 ml/1 tsp sunflower oil
1 small onion, finely chopped
400 g/14 oz cooked potato, mashed
225 g/8 oz cooked cabbage, finely shredded
4 slices of cooked beef, finely chopped
Salt and freshly ground black pepper

1 Gently heat the butter or margarine with the oil in a large, preferably non-stick, heavy-based frying pan (skillet) until melted. Add the onion and gently cook for 6–7 minutes until soft, but not coloured.

2 Add the potatoes, cabbage and beef. Cook over a medium heat for about 15 minutes or until lightly browned, stirring frequently.

3 Season generously with salt and pepper and serve.

🕐 **Preparation and cooking time:** 25 minutes

Shepherd's Pie

This is typical of a 'Tuesday' meal, made from the leftover cooked meat from the Sunday joint. Nowadays, such a dish would more commonly be made with raw meat. Cottage Pie is made in exactly the same way, using beef and beef stock. Whichever you choose, it makes a deliciously simple meal, served with any green vegetable.

SERVES 4

15 ml/1 tbsp sunflower oil
1 large onion, chopped
75 g/3 oz mushrooms, sliced
2 carrots, chopped
25 g/1 oz/¼ cup plain (all-purpose) flour
300 ml/½ pt/1¼ cups lamb stock
15 ml/1 tbsp tomato purée (paste)
1 bay leaf
350 g/12 oz/3 cups cold cooked lamb, finely chopped
30 ml/2 tbsp chopped fresh parsley
Salt and freshly ground black pepper
For the topping:
550 g/1¼ lb potatoes
25 g/1 oz/2 tbsp butter or margarine
45 ml/3 tbsp milk

1 Heat the oil in a large saucepan and gently fry (sauté) the onion for 10 minutes until soft. Add the mushrooms and carrots and cook for a further 2–3 minutes, or until the onions are just starting to colour.

2 Sprinkle over the flour, stir in and cook for a few seconds. Gradually stir in the stock. Bring to the boil, stirring all the time, until the mixture thickens.

3 Add the tomato purée and bay leaf. Cover and simmer gently for 15 minutes. Stir in the chopped meat, re-cover and simmer for a further 10 minutes.

4 Remove the bay leaf, stir in the parsley and season with salt and pepper, to taste. Spoon into a 1.75 litre/3 pt/7½ cup ovenproof serving dish.

5 Cut the potatoes into chunks and cook in boiling, salted water for 15 minutes or until tender. Drain and mash with the butter or margarine, milk, salt and pepper to taste. Spoon on top of the meat mixture.

6 Bake at 200°C/400°F/gas mark 6 for 20–25 minutes or until the meat mixture is bubbling and the topping golden brown.

🕐 **Preparation and cooking time:** 1¼ hours

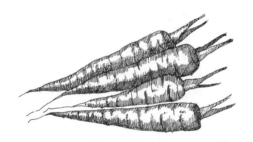

Cold Meat Pasties

Yet another way of dealing with leftovers from the Sunday roast! Unlike Cornish pasties, which require long, slow cooking, these should be cooked at a high temperature until the pastry (paste) is golden and the filling piping hot. Do not overcook, however, or they will be dry.

MAKES 6

For the pastry:
350 g/12 oz/3 cups plain (all-purpose) flour
A pinch of salt
100 g/4 oz/½ cup butter or margarine, diced
50 g/2 oz/¼ cup lard (shortening) or white vegetable fat
75–90 ml/5–6 tbsp cold water
For the filling:
350 g/12 oz/3 cups cold roast beef or lamb, trimmed and diced
225 g/8 oz cooked potato, diced
225 g/8 oz cooked root vegetables, such as carrots, swede (rutabaga) or parsnip, diced
45 ml/3 tbsp thick gravy
2.5 ml/½ tsp dried mixed herbs
Salt and freshly ground black pepper
A little beaten egg, to glaze

1 To make the pastry, sift the flour and salt into a mixing bowl. Rub in the butter or margarine and lard or white vegetable fat until the mixture resembles fine breadcrumbs.

2 Sprinkle the water over the dry ingredients and mix to a firm dough. Wrap in clingfilm (plastic wrap) and chill in the fridge for 30 minutes.

3 Divide the pastry into six pieces and roll out each on a lightly floured surface to a 20 cm/8 in round.

4 Mix together the meat, potato, root vegetables, gravy and herbs and season with salt and pepper. Spoon an equal amount on to one half of each pastry round.

5 Lightly brush the edges of the pastry with water, then fold the free half of each round over the filling. Press the edges together firmly to seal, then flute, or press the edges with the back of a fork to make a pattern.

6 Transfer the pasties to a baking (cookie) sheet and brush with beaten egg, to glaze. Make a steam-hole in the top of each.

7 Bake in a preheated oven at 220°C/425°F/gas mark 7 for 10 minutes, then turn down the oven to 180°C/350°C/ gas mark 4 and cook for a further 15–20 minutes or until the pastry is golden brown. Serve hot or warm.

🕐 **Preparation and cooking time:** 1 hour plus chilling

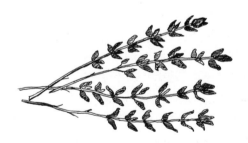

London Particular

Many years have passed since London was regularly smothered in dense fogs that were caused by coal fires and known as 'pea soupers' or 'London particulars', but this popular soup remains.

SERVES 6
350 g/12 oz/2 cups green split peas
10 ml/2 tsp sunflower oil
15 g/½ oz/1 tbsp butter or margarine
2 rashers (slices) of smoked streaky bacon, rinded and chopped
1 onion, chopped
1 carrot, chopped
1 celery stick, chopped
1.5 litres/2½ pts/6 cups ham or vegetable stock
1 bay leaf
Salt and freshly ground black pepper

1 Put the dried peas in a bowl, cover with plenty of cold water and leave to soak for at least 6 hours, or overnight. Drain well.

2 Heat the oil and butter or margarine in a saucepan until melted. Add the bacon and onion and cook for 5 minutes. Add the carrot and celery and cook for a further 2–3 minutes until beginning to soften.

3 Add the drained peas, stock and bay leaf. Bring to the boil, then cover and simmer for 1 hour until the peas are soft. Remove the bay leaf.

4 Allow to cool slightly, then purée in a food processor or blender until smooth. Return the soup to the rinsed-out pan, season to taste (you won't need salt if you've used ham stock) and reheat until piping hot. Serve in warmed soup bowls.

🕐 **Preparation and cooking time:** 1½ hours plus soaking

➤ **Cook's tip**
If you prefer slightly thinner soup, dilute it with a little extra stock, or milk for a creamier texture.

I asked him whether there was a great fire anywhere. For the streets were so full of dense brown smoke that scarcely anything was to be seen. 'O dear no, miss,' he said. 'This is a London particular.' I had never heard of such a thing. 'A fog, miss,' said the young gentleman.

Charles Dickens, *Bleak House*

Thick Vegetable Soup

This soup was made with whatever vegetables were to hand, but is best made with root vegetables, such as potatoes, onions, carrots and leeks.

SERVES 6
700 g/1½ lb mixed vegetables (see above)
40 g/1½ oz/3 tbsp butter or margarine
1.2 litres/2 pts/5 cups vegetable stock
A few sprigs of parsley
1 bay leaf
A sprig of thyme
150 ml/¼ pt/⅔ cup milk
Salt and freshly ground black pepper

1 Prepare the vegetables and cut into 2.5 cm/1 in pieces. Melt the butter or margarine in a large saucepan, add the vegetables and gently cook for 5–6 minutes, stirring.

2 Add the stock and herbs and bring to the boil. Cover and simmer gently for 30–40 minutes or until the vegetables are very tender.

3 Remove the bay leaf and thyme and purée the soup in a food processor or blender until smooth (you may have to do this in two batches). Return to the saucepan, stir in the milk and season with salt and pepper.

4 Reheat, then ladle into warmed soup bowls.

🕐 **Preparation and cooking time:** 1 hour

Corned Beef Pie

SERVES 4

For the pastry (paste):
350 g/12 oz/3 cups plain (all-purpose) flour
A pinch of salt
1.5 ml/¼ tsp mustard powder
100 g/4 oz/½ cup butter or margarine, diced
50 g/2 oz/¼ cup lard (shortening) or white fat, diced
75–90 ml/5–6 tbsp cold water
For the filling:
15 g/½ oz/1 tbsp butter or margarine
1 small onion, finely chopped
175 g/6 oz cooked diced vegetables, such as carrots, green
    beans or peas
225 g/8 oz/1 small can of corned beef, finely chopped
Salt and freshly ground black pepper
4 eggs
A little beaten egg or milk, to glaze

1 To make the pastry, sift the flour, salt and mustard powder into a bowl. Rub in the butter or margarine and lard or white fat until the mixture resembles breadcrumbs.

2 Sprinkle the water over the dry ingredients and mix to a firm dough. Wrap in clingfilm (plastic wrap) and chill in the fridge for 30 minutes.

3 Meanwhile, make the filling. Melt the butter or margarine in a frying pan (skillet) and cook the onion for 10 minutes until very soft. Remove the pan from the heat and stir in the vegetables and corned beef. Season with salt and pepper.

4 Roll out two-thirds of the pastry and use to line a deep 20 cm/8 in flan tin (pie pan). Spoon in the filling and make four slight hollows with a spoon.

5 Crack open the eggs, one at a time, and separate the yolks from the whites. Put a yolk into each of the hollows. Whisk the egg whites with a fork, then pour over the flan.

6 Roll out the remaining pastry, dampen the edges and place over the pie. Roll over the top with a rolling pin to seal the edge and to remove excess pastry from the sides.

7 Brush the top of the pie with beaten egg or milk, then bake in a preheated oven at 200°C/400°F/gas mark 6 for 15 minutes. Lower the oven temperature to 180°C/350°F/gas mark 4 and bake for a further 15 minutes.

8 Leave to settle and cool in the flan tin for 5 minutes, then carefully remove and cut into slices to serve.

⊙ **Preparation and cooking time:** 1 hour 10 minutes

Woolton Pie

During the Second World War, Lord Woolton became the Minister of Food and this vegetable pie with a potato crust was named after him. Any available seasonal vegetables were used in the filling.

SERVES 6

For the pastry (paste):
100 g/4 oz floury potatoes, diced
225 g/8 oz/2 cups plain (all-purpose) flour
100 g/4 oz/½ cup chilled butter or margarine, diced
1 egg, beaten

For the filling:
25 g/1 oz/2 tbsp butter or margarine
225 g/8 oz leeks, trimmed and sliced
225 g/8 oz carrots, diced
225 g/8 oz Brussels sprouts, quartered
25 g/1 oz/¼ cup plain (all-purpose) flour
300 ml/½ pt/1¼ cups milk
Salt and freshly ground black pepper

1 To make the pastry, cook the potatoes in boiling, salted water for 15 minutes, or until tender. Drain well and mash until smooth.

2 Sift the flour into a bowl. Rub in the butter or margarine until the mixture resembles breadcrumbs.

3 Mix together the mashed potato and about half the beaten egg, reserving the remainder for glazing. Add to the dry ingredients and mix to a dough, adding a few drops of water if the mixture is too dry. Wrap in clingfilm (plastic wrap) and chill for at least 30 minutes.

4 Meanwhile, make the filling. Melt the butter or margarine in a large saucepan and cook the leeks and carrots over a medium heat for 5 minutes. Add the Brussels sprouts and cook for a further 2 minutes.

5 Sprinkle over the flour and stir in. Remove from the heat, then gradually mix in the milk. Bring to the boil, stirring all the time until thickened. Season to taste, then spoon into a large pie dish and leave to cool.

6 Roll out the pastry on a lightly floured surface to a round 5 cm/2 in larger than the dish. Cut off a 2.5 cm/1 in strip from around the edge. Dampen the rim of the pie dish and position the pastry strip on it. Brush with water.

7 Lift the pastry lid into position and press the edges together to seal. Trim off excess pastry, then flute the edges.

8 Brush with the reserved beaten egg to glaze and make a steam-hole in the centre of the pie. Place on a baking (cookie) tray and cook in a preheated oven at 200°C/400°F/ gas mark 6 for 35–40 minutes, or until the pastry is golden brown. Serve hot.

⏱ **Preparation and cooking time:** 2 hours

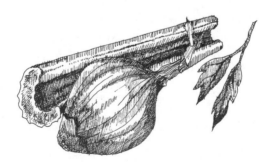

Mock Crab

This was created during Victorian times and uses chicken, cheese and hard-boiled (hard-cooked) eggs to resemble the white and brown meat of a cooked crab.

SERVES 2

1 hard-boiled egg, shelled
2.5 ml/½ tsp made English mustard
A few drops of anchovy essence (extract)
100 g/4 oz/1 cup Cheddar cheese, finely grated
2 small cooked skinless chicken breasts, finely chopped
Lettuce leaves, slices of cucumber and wedges of lemon, to garnish
Brown bread and butter, to serve

1 Separate the egg into white and yolk. Chop the white very finely. Reserve about half of the yolk and mash the rest in a small bowl with the mustard and anchovy essence.

2 Add the cheese and chicken to the yolk mixture. Mix well and season to taste. Cover and chill in the fridge for 1 hour.

3 Spoon the mixture into cleaned crab shells and arrange on a few lettuce leaves on individual serving plates. (If you have no shells, simply pile the mixture straight on to the lettuce leaves.) Arrange a row of sliced cucumber down the middle of each.

4 Press the reserved egg yolk through a fine sieve (strainer). Sprinkle alternate rows of yolk and egg white on either side of the cucumber.

5 Carefully cover and chill until ready to serve. Garnish with wedges of lemon to squeeze over and serve with thinly sliced brown bread and butter.

⏱ **Preparation time:** 30 minutes plus chilling

Oat Pancakes

Rationing in Britain lasted until 1954, well beyond the end of the Second World War. During 1946 there were fears of a world famine and for the first time bread was rationed. Oats, which grew mainly in Scotland, were heavily subsidised by the government, so recipes using them were common.

MAKES 8

50 g/2 oz/½ cup plain (all-purpose) flour
A pinch of salt
50 g/2 oz/½ cup rolled oats
1 egg
300 ml/½ pt/1¼ cups milk
30 ml/2 tbsp sunflower oil
Wedges of lemon and caster (superfine) sugar or golden (light corn) syrup, to serve

1 Sift the flour and salt together into a food processor or blender. Add the oats, egg, milk and 5 ml/1 tsp of the oil. Blend to a smooth batter.

2 Pour into a jug, and leave to stand for about 20 minutes, so that the oats absorb some of the liquid.

3 Heat a 18 cm/7 in frying pan (skillet), then brush with a little oil. Stir the batter, then pour a small amount into the hot pan and swirl around to spread thinly over the base.

4 Cook over a moderate to high heat for about 1 minute or until the underside is golden. Flip the pancake over and cook the other side for 45 seconds to 1 minute.

5 Slide the pancake out on to a sheet of greaseproof (waxed) paper, cover and keep warm. Repeat until all the batter has been used up, lightly oiling the pan each time and stacking up the pancakes as they are made.

6 Serve straight away with wedges of lemon and caster sugar or golden syrup.

⏲ **Preparation and cooking time:** 25 minutes plus standing

Bread and Butter Pudding

This dessert was originally designed as a way to use up stale bread. Cold tea was traditionally used to plump the fruit, but brandy gives a better flavour!

SERVES 6

75 g/3 oz/½ cup mixed dried fruit
30 ml/2 tbsp cold tea or brandy
6 thick slices of white bread, crusts removed, if preferred
50 g/2 oz/¼ cup butter or margarine
3 eggs
50 g/2 oz/¼ cup caster (superfine) sugar
750 ml/1¼ pts/3 cups milk
15 ml/1 tbsp demerara sugar
2.5 ml/½ tsp ground cinnamon

1 Put the dried fruit in a small bowl and pour over the tea or brandy. Stir and leave to soak while preparing the bread.

2 Spread the slices of bread generously with butter or margarine and cut into triangles. Arrange a layer of bread over the base of a 1.5 litre/2½ pt/6 cup greased, shallow ovenproof dish.

3 Scatter the fruit and any remaining liquid over the bread, then arrange the remaining bread neatly on top of the fruit.

4 Beat together the eggs and caster sugar, then stir in the milk. Slowly pour over the bread and leave to soak for about 5 minutes.

5 Push the bread down into the egg and milk mixture, then sprinkle the top evenly with demerara sugar and ground cinnamon.

6 Place the dish in a roasting tin (pan) and pour in enough hot water to come halfway up the sides. Bake at 180°C/350°F/gas mark 4 for about 45 minutes or until lightly set and golden brown.

⏱ **Preparation and cooking time:** 1¼ hours

Dripping Cake

The fat from a roasted joint was always saved. It separated out into a layer of rich jelly and a layer of fat and was spread on bread or toast. It could also be clarified (see Cook's tip, below) and used in baking, as in this plain fruit cake.

CUTS INTO 9 SQUARES

225 g/8 oz/2 cups self-raising (self-rising) flour
2.5 ml/½ tsp mixed (apple-pie) spice
A pinch of salt
100 g/4 oz/1 cup clarified dripping, butter or margarine
75 g/3 oz/⅓ cup caster (superfine) sugar
175 g/6 oz/1 cup dried mixed fruit (fruit cake mix)
1 egg, lightly beaten
100 ml/3½ fl oz/scant ½ cup milk

1 Sift the flour, spice and salt into a mixing bowl. Rub in the dripping until the mixture resembles breadcrumbs. Stir in the sugar and dried fruit. Make a well in the middle.

2 Mix the egg and milk, then mix into the dry ingredients.

3 Spoon the mixture into a greased and lined 15 cm/6 in square cake tin (pan) and level the top.

4 Bake at 180°C/350°F/gas mark 4 for about 50 minutes until a skewer inserted into the middle comes out clean.

5 Leave in the tin for 15 minutes before turning out on to a wire rack to cool. When cold, wrap in greaseproof (waxed) paper, then in foil, and store in a cool place.

⏲ **Preparation and cooking time:** 1½ hours

➤ **Cook's tip**
To clarify dripping, put it into a saucepan with 150 ml/¼ pt/ ⅔ cup cold water. Slowly bring to the boil, skimming off any scum. Strain into a bowl and leave to cool, then chill. Carefully lift off the fat and remove any jelly from the bottom. Heat the fat gently for a few minutes to evaporate any water. Pour into a bowl and chill.

Preserves and Pickles

Cockneys love strongly flavoured foods. There would always be a few jars in the larder, containing pickled onions, red cabbage and piccalilli, made in the autumn when the basic ingredients were cheap. Pickled eggs and 'wallies' – small pickled cucumbers – were, perhaps surprisingly, first introduced by the Polish and Russian Jews who settled in the East End at the beginning of the twentieth century, but were quickly adopted by the locals and are still sold in fish and chip shops.

Sweet preserves were popular too, especially if they could be made from free ingredients, such as hedgerow fruit. One day a year, the whole family would take a trip to the country. This might be to Kent, Middlesex or Essex and would often include an afternoon of gathering blackberries, also known as brambles, and other fruit, such as elderberries and crab apples. The jams (conserves) they made would be spread on bread for Sunday tea or used for turning leftover scraps of dough into tarts.

Pickled Onions

MAKES 900 G/2 LB
900 g/2 lb pickling onions, unpeeled
225 g/8 oz/2 cups salt
For the spiced vinegar:
600 ml/1 pt/2½ cups malt vinegar
10 ml/2 tsp whole allspice
5 ml/1 tsp whole cloves
4 black peppercorns
1 bay leaf

1 Place the unpeeled onions in a large bowl. Put half the salt in a saucepan with 1.2 litres/2 pts/5 cups water and heat gently, stirring occasionally until the salt has dissolved. Pour over the onions, cover and leave to soak for 12 hours.

2 Drain the onions, peel off the skins and return to the bowl. Dissolve the remaining salt in 1.2 litres/2 pts/5 cups water as before. Pour over the peeled onions and leave for a further 24 hours.

3 Put the vinegar, spices and bay leaf in a saucepan and bring to the boil. Turn off the heat, cover and leave to marinate for 2 hours. Strain the cooled, spiced vinegar into a jug.

4 Drain the onions and rinse well. Pack them into sterilised jars, then pour over the spiced vinegar to cover the onions completely. Seal the tops with vinegar-proof lids.

5 Store the pickled onions in a cool, dark place for at least 2 months before serving. Use within 1 year of making.

⊕ **Preparation time:** 30 minutes plus soaking

➤ **Cook's tip**
To make pickled red cabbage, layer 1.5 kg/3 lb of finely shredded red cabbage with 2 sliced onions and 45 ml/3 tbsp salt. Leave for 24 hours, then rinse, drain and pack in jars with spiced vinegar. You will need about four times the quantity given above. Use within a month.

Piccalilli

This pickle could be made from almost any mixture of low-priced vegetables. Prepare the vegetables before weighing – finely dice marrow and cucumber and remove the seeds; cut cauliflower into tiny florets and slice beans into 1 cm/½ in pieces. It lasts for about a year.

MAKES 1.5 KG/3 LB

1.5 kg/3 lb prepared mixture of marrow, cucumber, cauliflower and beans (see above)
175 g/6 oz salt
750 ml/1¼ pts/3 cups distilled vinegar
175 g/6 oz/¾ cup granulated sugar
10 ml/2 tsp English mustard powder
5 ml/1 tsp ground ginger
2 garlic cloves, crushed
20 g/¾ oz/1½ tbsp plain (all-purpose) flour
15 ml/1 tbsp ground turmeric

1 Layer the vegetables in a large bowl, sprinkling salt between the layers. Pour over 1.75 litres/3 pts/7½ cups of cold water and leave to soak for 24 hours.

2 Drain the vegetables, rinse, then drain again.

3 Reserve 100 ml/3½ fl oz/scant ½ cup of the vinegar. Put the remainder in a large, stainless steel preserving pan with the sugar, mustard, ginger and garlic. Heat gently until the sugar has dissolved.

4 Add the vegetables, bring to the boil, then reduce the heat and simmer gently, uncovered, for 20 minutes until the vegetables are just cooked, but still crisp.

5 Blend the flour and turmeric with the reserved vinegar and add to the vegetables. Bring to the boil, stirring all the time, and simmer for 2 minutes.

6 Spoon into sterilised jars and cover with vinegar-proof tops. Store in a cool, dark place for at least 2 weeks.

☉ **Preparation and cooking time:** 45 minutes plus soaking

Pickled Eggs

These are sold as a traditional accompaniment to fish and chips (fries) but are also delicious with curries and spiced rice dishes. For the latter, you can add a little fresh root ginger, peeled and chopped, and a couple of dried red chillies to the vinegar. They can also be made with dainty quails' eggs.

MAKES 12
12 hard-boiled (hard-cooked) eggs
15 ml/1 tbsp mixed peppercorns
10 ml/2 tsp salt
900 ml/1½ pts/3¾ cups cider or white wine vinegar

1 Shell the eggs and pack into sterilised jars. Put the remaining ingredients in a saucepan and bring to the boil. Lower the heat, cover and simmer for 2 minutes.

2 Turn off the heat and leave while the vinegar cools and the flavours infuse.

3 Strain the vinegar over the eggs, to cover completely. If there isn't quite enough, add a little extra vinegar.

4 Cover with vinegar-proof tops and store in a cool, dark place for at least 2 days before serving. Use within 6 months of making.

⊕ **Preparation and cooking time:** 10 minutes plus soaking

Chunky Autumn Chutney

Although there was little land for growing vegetables in the East End, many cockneys prided themselves on having a patch of land on the allotments in the Tottenham and Hackney marshes to the north or Greenwich and Erith to the south. At the end of the growing season, surplus fruit and vegetables, including half-ripened and green tomatoes, could be turned into tasty chutneys.

MAKES 3.2 KG/7 LB

450 g/1 lb onions
450 g/1 lb ripe or green tomatoes, skinned, if preferred
450 g/1 lb plums
450 g/1 lb eating or cooking (dessert or tart) apples
2 cloves garlic, crushed
350 g/12 oz/2 cups sultanas (golden raisins)
600 ml/1 pt/2½ cups white or red wine vinegar
5 ml/1 tsp ground ginger
A large pinch of mixed (apple-pie) spice
450 g/1 lb/2 cups demerara sugar

1 Roughly chop the onions and tomatoes. Halve and stone (pit) the plums. Quarter, core, peel and roughly chop the apples. Put in a large, stainless steel or preserving pan.

2 Add all the remaining ingredients except the sugar. Simmer, uncovered, for 30 minutes or until the fruit and vegetables are tender.

3 Add the sugar to the pan and stir until dissolved. Simmer gently, stirring frequently, for about 10 minutes or until very thick.

4 Allow the chutney to cool until tepid, then pot in sterilised jars, making sure that it is well packed down. Cover with waxed discs and vinegar-proof lids.

5 Store in a cool dark place for at least 1 month before eating. Use within 18 months of making.

🕐 **Preparation and cooking time:** 1 hour

Bramble Jam

This preserve has a very fresh, fruity flavour because of the short cooking time. Make it in the autumn when you have picked some hedgerow blackberries.

MAKES 900 G/2 LB
450 g/1 lb blackberries
450 g/1 lb/2 cups preserving sugar with pectin

1 Briefly rinse the blackberries in a large colander and drain thoroughly. Put in a preserving pan with the sugar.

2 Slowly bring to boiling point, gently stirring occasionally to make sure that the sugar has dissolved.

3 Boil rapidly for 3 minutes, then remove from the heat. Put a teaspoonful on a saucer and leave to cool. If it wrinkles when pushed with your finger, it has reached setting point. If not, boil for a little longer and test again. Pot straight away in warm, dry sterilised jars, then cover.

4 Store the jam (conserve) in a cool, dark place and use within 1 year of making.

⏲ **Preparation and cooking time:** 15 minutes

Elderberry Jelly

This jewel-bright jelly (clear conserve) is equally good served as an accompaniment to roasted meats or spread on bread, toast or scones (biscuits). Cockneys would collect the elderberries on their country outings at the end of the summer.

MAKES ABOUT 700 G/1½ LB

900 g/2 lb elderberries
900 ml/1½ pts/3¾ cups water
About 900 g/2 lb/4 cups preserving or granulated sugar

1 Strip the fruit off the stalks, using the prongs of a fork, and place in a large pan. Pour over the water and bring to the boil. Simmer for 15 minutes or until very tender.

2 Mash the fruit to extract all the juices, then spoon the pulp into a jelly bag suspended over a large bowl and leave to drip through for at least 4 hours. Do not squeeze the bag or the jelly will be cloudy. Discard the pulp in the bag.

3 Measure the liquid and for every 600 ml/1 pt/2½ cups, add 450 g/1 lb/2 cups sugar. Gently heat, stirring frequently until the sugar has dissolved.

4 Bring to the boil, then boil rapidly for about 10 minutes until it reaches setting point of 105°C/221°F. (If you do not have a thermometer, test for setting point by putting a teaspoonful of jelly on a cold plate; it should form a skin that wrinkles when pushed with your finger.)

5 Take the pan off the heat and remove any scum with a slotted spoon. Pour into warm, sterilised jars and cover with a waxed disc. When cold, cover the jars with dampened cellophane and secure with an elastic band.

⊕ **Preparation and cooking time:** 45 minutes plus draining

➤ **Cook's tip**
You can make crab apple jelly in the same way to serve with game, pork or chicken.

Damson Cheese

Fruit cheeses are a good way of using up fruit when there is a glut and, unlike jellies (clear conserves), they use the fruit pulp, so nothing is wasted. They're called 'cheeses' because they are cooked to a stiff consistency, then turned out and sliced. Damsons work particularly well, but apples, blackberries, blackcurrants, cherries, gooseberries, plums and quinces are also suitable for preserving this way.

MAKES ABOUT 900 G/2 LB
450 g/1 lb damsons, halved and stoned (pitted)
150 ml/¼ pt/⅔ cups water
About 450 g/1 lb/2 cups preserving sugar
Glycerine or flavourless oil, for greasing

1 Put the damsons and water into a preserving pan and simmer very gently until soft. Purée in a blender or food processor, then pass through a sieve (strainer) to remove any pieces of skin.

2 Weigh the pulp, then return to the pan, bring to the boil and simmer for 5–10 minutes until you have a dry paste. Stir frequently to prevent it sticking.

3 For every 450 g/1 lb fruit pulp, add 450 g/1 lb/2 cups sugar. Heat very gently, stirring until the sugar has dissolved, then continue to heat and stir for 5 minutes.

4 Grease small, clean containers with a little glycerine or a flavourless oil, such as almond, to allow you to turn the cheese out when set. Pot, cover and seal.

5 Store the cheese in a cool, dark place and use within 1 year of making. To unmould, dip the jar briefly in warm water, then turn the cheese out on to a plate to serve.

🕑 **Preparation and cooking time:** 40 minutes

Orange and Lemon Curd

Any surplus citrus fruit brought into the London docks was sold cheaply by the costermongers.

MAKES 900 G/2 LB
Finely grated rind and juice of 3 lemons
Finely grated rind and juice of 1 small orange
4 eggs, beaten
100 g/4 oz/½ cup butter
350 g/12 oz/1½ cups caster (superfine) sugar

1 Put all the ingredients in a double boiler or in a heatproof bowl set over a pan of gently simmering water. Stir frequently until the sugar has dissolved.

2 Continue cooking for about 20 minutes, or until the mixture is thick enough to coat the back of the spoon. Take care not to let it boil or it will curdle.

3 Strain through a fine sieve (strainer) into a warm jug. Pour into sterilised jars, cover with waxed discs and lids. Store in the fridge and use within 3 weeks.

⏱ **Preparation and cooking time:** 40 minutes

Oranges and lemons,' say the bells of St Clements.
'I owe you five farthings,' say the bells of St Martins.
'When will you pay me?' say the bells of Old Bailey.
'When I grow rich,' say the bells of Shoreditch.
'When will that be?' say the bells of Stepney.
'I'm sure I don't know,' says the great bell of Bow.

Traditional nursery rhyme

Index